HOW TO
TEPS

점수대별 TEPS 실전 모의고사

실 전 력
Level 3

How to TEPS 실전력 Level 3

지은이 넥서스 TEPS연구소
펴낸이 안용백
펴낸곳 (주)도서출판 넥서스

출판신고 1992년 4월 3일 제311-2002-2호 ①

121-840 서울시 마포구 서교동 394-2
Tel (02)330-5500 Fax (02)330-5555

ISBN 978-89-5797-419-3 18740

저자와 출판사의 허락없이 내용의 일부를 인용하거나
발췌하는 것을 금합니다.

가격은 뒤표지에 있습니다.
잘못 만들어진 책은 구입처에서 바꾸어 드립니다.

본책은 〈How to TEPS 실전력 700〉의 문제집으로만
재구성하였습니다.

www.nexusEDU.kr
NEXUS Edu는 (주)도서출판 넥서스의 초·중·고 학습물 전문 브랜드입니다.

텝스 상급 진입을 위한 최적의 실전 모의고사

HOW TO
TEPS

넥서스 TEPS연구소 지음

점수대별 TEPS 실전 모의고사

실전력
Level 3

NEXUS Edu

Preface

1999년 1월 첫 TEPS 정기시험 시행 이후 100회를 훌쩍 넘으면서 TEPS는 이제 명실공히 한국인의 영어능력을 가장 객관적이면서 과학적으로 테스팅하는 시험으로 자리매김을 하였습니다.

TEPS 시험 유형을 자세히 분석해 보면 기존의 영어능력 검정시험과 확연히 다른 두 가지 점을 파악할 수 있을 겁니다. 문법과 어휘 영역에서 문어체 표현뿐만 아니라 구어체 표현까지 다양하게 출시된다는 것과 테스팅 타임(2시간 20분) 동안 처리해야 할 문제 정보량이 너무나 방대하기 때문에 TEPS만의 독특한 문제 유형에 익숙해지지 않으면 시간 안에 주어진 문제를 다 풀기가 버겁다는 것입니다. 따라서 TEPS 문제 유형에 익숙해지도록, 소위 말해서 전천후 TEPS 체질로 영어 공부 환경을 완전히 바꾸어야 TEPS 시험에서 고득점을 얻을 수 있습니다.

이러한 문제 유형 파악을 위해 단시간에 가장 효과적인 학습 방법은 시험 출제 경향과 유사한 문제들을 많이 경험하는 것이라는 것을 TEPS를 준비해 본 수험생이라면 누구나 알 것입니다. 시중에 TEPS 모의고사 문제집은 이미 많이 나와 있지만 수험생 각자의 학업 성취 목표에 따라 난이도를 제대로 조절한 모의고사 교재는 아직 없는 것을 발견하고 이번에 넥서스 TEPS연구소 연구원들이 난이도별 모의고사 시리즈를 개발하게 됐습니다.

보다 TEPS 기출문제와 유사한 문제들을 개발하기 위해 연구원들 전원 수시로 TEPS 시험에 응시하며 데이터를 정리했으며, 매력적인 지문과 질문 개발을 위해 미국에 있는 Henry J. Amen Ⅳ, 뉴질랜드 출신의 Anne Cave 교수님 외 국내외 여러 박사님들이 끝까지 많은 도움을 주셨습니다. 이 책의 청해 문제 녹음을 위해 가는 날 이 땅에 예상치 않은 함박눈이 쏟아져 연구원들이 무지 고생했던 추억이 있답니다. 하루라도 독자들에게 먼저 다가가기 위해 모든 외부 환경 요소들을 뛰어넘어 이제 〈How to TEPS 실력력 Level 3〉를 이 세상에 내놓게 됐습니다. TEPS 상급 진입이 독자들에게 또 다른 새로운 도전과 꿈을 향한 전진이 될 것입니다. TEPS 이상의 비전 성취를 준비하는 수험생들에게 본책이 유익한 동반자가 될 수 있기를 바랍니다.

넥서스 TEPS연구소 연구원 일동

Contents

Preface   5

TEPS Q & A   8

All about the TEPS   10

Actual **Test 1**

Listening Comprehension   19

Grammar   23

Vocabulary   31

Reading Comprehension   39

Actual **Test 2**

Listening Comprehension   57

Grammar   61

Vocabulary   69

Reading Comprehension   77

Actual **Test 3**

Listening Comprehension   95

Grammar   99

Vocabulary   107

Reading Comprehension   115

Actual **Test 1** Scripts   132

Actual **Test 2** Scripts   142

Actual **Test 3** Scripts   152

Actual **Test 1** Answer Keys   162

Actual **Test 2** Answer Keys   163

Actual **Test 3** Answer Keys   164

TEPS 등급표   165

i **-TEPS Review**   166

TEPS Q & A

1 / TEPS란?

❶ Test of English Proficiency developed by Seoul National University의 약자로 서울대학교 언어교육원에서 개발하고, TEPS관리위원회에서 주관하는 국가공인 영어시험

❷ 1999년 1월 처음 시행 이후 2010년 11월 현재 128회 실시했으며, 연 16회 실시

❸ 정부기관 및 기업의 직원 채용, 인사고과, 해외 파견 근무자 선발과 더불어 대학과 특목고 입학 및 졸업 자격 요건, 국가고시 및 자격 시험의 영어 대체 시험으로 활용

❹ 100여 명의 국내외 유수 대학의 최고 수준 영어 전문가들이 출제하고, 언어 테스팅 분야의 세계적인 권위자인 Bachman 교수(미국 UCLA)와 Oller 교수(미국 뉴멕시코대)로부터 타당성을 검증받음

❺ 말하기·쓰기 시험인 TEPS Speaking & Writing도 별도로 실시 중이며, 2009년 10월부터 이를 통합한 *i*-TEPS 실시

2 / TEPS 시험 구성

영역	Part별 내용	문항수	시간/배점
청해 Listening Comprehension	Part I : 문장 하나를 듣고 이어질 대화 고르기 Part II : 3문장의 대화를 듣고 이어질 대화 고르기 Part III : 6~8 문장의 대화를 듣고 질문에 해당하는 답 고르기 Part IV : 담화문의 내용을 듣고 질문에 해당하는 답 고르기	15 15 15 15	55분 400점
문법 Grammar	Part I : 대화문의 빈칸에 적절한 표현 고르기 Part II : 문장의 빈칸에 적절한 표현 고르기 Part III : 대화에서 어법상 틀리거나 어색한 부분 고르기 Part IV : 단문에서 문법상 틀리거나 어색한 부분 고르기	20 20 5 5	25분 100점
어휘 Vocabulary	Part I : 대화문의 빈칸에 적절한 단어 고르기 Part II : 단문의 빈칸에 적절한 단어 고르기	25 25	15분 100점
독해 Reading Comprehension	Part I : 지문을 읽고 빈칸에 들어갈 내용 고르기 Part II : 지문을 읽고 질문에 가장 적절한 내용 고르기 Part III : 지문을 읽고 문맥상 어색한 내용 고르기	16 21 3	45분 400점
총계	13개 Parts	200	140분 990점

☆ **IRT** (Item Response Theory)에 의하여 최고점이 990점, 최저점이 10점으로 조정됨.

3 / TEPS 시험 응시 정보

현장 접수
❶ www.teps.or.kr에서 인근 접수처 확인
❷ 준비물: 응시료 33,000원(현금만 가능), 증명사진 1매(3×4 cm)
❸ 접수처 방문: 해당 접수기간 평일 오전 10시 ~ 오후 5시

인터넷 접수
❶ TEPS관리위원회 홈페이지 접속 www.teps.or.kr
❷ 준비물: 스캔한 사진 파일, 응시료 결제를 위한 신용카드 및 은행 계좌
❸ 응시료: 33,000원(일반) / 17,000원(군인) / 36,000원(추가 접수)

4 / TEPS 시험 당일 정보

❶ 고사장 입실 완료: 9시 30분(일요일) / 3시(토요일)
❷ 준비물: 신분증, 컴퓨터용 사인펜, 수정테이프, 수험표, 시계
❸ 유효한 신분증
  성인: 주민등록증, 운전면허증, 여권, 공무원증, 현역간부 신분증, 군무원증, 주민등록증 발급 신청 확인서, 외국인 등록증
  초·중고생: 학생증, 여권, 청소년증, 주민등록증, 주민등록증 발급 신청 확인서, TEPS 신분확인 증명서
❹ 시험 시간: 2시간 20분 (중간에 쉬는 시간 없음, 각 영역별 제한시간 엄수)
❺ 성적 확인: 약 2주 후 인터넷에서 조회 가능

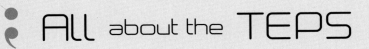

All about the TEPS

Choose the most appropriate response to the statement. (15문항)

문제유형　질의 응답 문제를 다루며 한 번만 들려주고, 내용은 일상의 구어체 표현으로 구성되어 있다.

> W　I wish my French were as good as yours.
> M　_____

(a) Yes, I'm going to visit France.
✔ (b) Thanks, but I still have a lot to learn.
(c) I hope it works out that way.
(d) You can say that again.

번역　W　당신처럼 프랑스어를 잘하면 좋을 텐데요.
　　　　M　_____

(a) 네, 프랑스를 방문할 예정이에요.
(b) 고마워요. 하지만 아직도 배울 게 많아요.
(c) 그렇게 잘 되기를 바라요.
(d) 당신 말이 맞아요.

Choose the most appropriate response to complete the conversation. (15문항)

문제유형　두 사람이 A–B–A–B 순으로 대화하는 형식이며, 한 번만 들려준다.

> W　I wish I earned more money.
> M　You could change jobs.
> W　But I love the field I work in.
> M　_____

(a) I think it would be better.
✔ (b) Ask for a raise then.
(c) You should have a choice in it.
(d) I'm not that interested in money.

번역　W　돈을 더 많이 벌면 좋을 텐데요.
　　　　M　직장을 바꾸지 그래요?
　　　　W　하지만 난 지금 일하고 있는 분야가 좋아요.
　　　　M　_____

(a) 더 좋아질 거라고 생각해요.
(b) 그러면 급여를 올려 달라고 말해요.
(c) 그 안에서 선택권이 있어야 해요.
(d) 돈에 그렇게 관심이 있지는 않아요.

Choose the option that best answers the question. (15문항)

문제유형   비교적 긴 대화문. 대화문과 질문은 두 번, 선택지는 한 번 들려준다.

> M   Hello. You're new here, aren't you?
> W   Yes, it's my second week. I'm Karen.
> M   What department are you in?
> W   Customer service, on the first floor.
> M   I see. I'm in sales.
> W   So, you'll be working on commission, then.
> M   Yes. I like that, but it's very stressful sometimes.

Q: Which is correct according to the conversation?
(a) The man and woman work in the same department.
✔ (b) The woman works in the customer service department.
(c) The man thinks the woman's job is stressful.
(d) The woman likes working for commissions.

번역   M   안녕하세요. 새로 오신 분이시죠?
W   예, 여기 온 지 2주째예요. 전 캐런이에요.
M   어느 부서에서 근무하시나요?
W   1층 고객 지원부에서 일해요.
M   그렇군요. 전 영업부에서 일해요.
W   그러면 커미션제로 일하시는군요.
M   네. 좋기는 하지만 가끔은 스트레스를 많이 받아요.

Q: 대화에 따르면 옳은 것은?
(a) 남자와 여자는 같은 부서에서 일한다.
(b) 여자는 고객 지원부에서 일한다.
(c) 남자는 여자의 일이 스트레스가 많다고 생각한다.
(d) 여자는 커미션제로 일하는 것을 좋아한다.

 All about the TEPS

 PART IV

Choose the option that best answers the question. (15문항)

문제유형   담화문의 주제, 세부 사항, 사실 여부 및 이를 근거로 한 추론 등을 다룬다.

> Confucian tradition placed an emphasis on the values of the group over the individual. It also taught that workers should not question authority. This helped industrialization by creating a pliant populace willing to accept long hours and low wages and not question government policies. The lack of dissent helped to produce stable government and this was crucial for investment and industrialization in East Asian countries.

Q: What can be inferred from the lecture?
(a) Confucianism promoted higher education in East Asia.
(b) East Asian people accept poverty as a Confucian virtue.
✔ (c) Confucianism fostered industrialization in East Asia.
(d) East Asian countries are used to authoritarian rule.

번역   유교 전통은 개인보다 조직의 가치를 강조했습니다. 또한 노동자들에게 권위에 대해 의문을 제기하지 말라고 가르쳤습니다. 이것은 장시간 노동과 저임금을 기꺼이 감수하고 정부의 정책에 의문을 제기하지 않는 고분고분한 민중을 만들어 냄으로써 산업화에 도움이 되었습니다. 반대의 부재는 안정적인 정부를 만드는 데 도움이 되었고, 이는 동아시아 국가들에서 투자와 산업화에 결정적이었습니다.

Q: 강의로부터 유추할 수 있는 것은?
(a) 유교는 동아시아에서 고등교육을 장려했다.
(b) 동아시아 사람들은 유교의 미덕으로 가난을 받아들인다.
(c) 유교는 동아시아에서 산업화를 촉진했다.
(d) 동아시아 국가들은 독재주의 법칙에 익숙하다.

Grammar 50문항

PART I Choose the best answer for the blank. (20문항)

문제유형 A, B 두 사람의 짧은 대화 중에 빈칸이 있다. 동사의 시제 및 수 일치, 문장의 어순 등이 주로 출제되며, 구어체 문법의 독특한 표현들을 숙지하고 있어야 한다.

> A Should I just keep waiting _____ me back?
> B Well, just waiting doesn't get anything done, does it?

(a) for the editor write
✔ (b) until the editor writes
(c) till the editor writing
(d) that the editor writes

번역 A 편집자가 나한테 답장을 쓸 때까지 기다리고만 있어야 합니까?
B 글쎄요, 단지 기다리고 있다고 해서 무슨 일이 이루어지는 건 아니겠죠?

PART II Choose the best answer for the blank. (20문항)

문제유형 문어체 문장을 읽고 어법상 빈칸에 적절한 표현을 고르는 유형으로 세부적인 문법 자체에 대한 이해는 물론 구문에 대한 이해력도 테스트한다.

> All passengers should remain seated at _____ times.

(a) any
(b) some
✔ (c) all
(d) each

번역 모든 승객들은 항상 앉아 있어야 합니다.

13

All about the TEPS

PART III **Identify the option that contains an awkward expression or an error in grammar.** (5문항)

문제유형 대화문에서 어법상 틀리거나 어색한 부분이 있는 문장을 고르는 문제로 구성되어 있다.

> (a) A Where did you go on your honeymoon?
> (b) B We flew to Bali, Indonesia.
> ✔ (c) A Did you have good time?
> (d) B Sure. It was a lot of fun.

번역
(a) A 신혼여행은 어디로 가셨나요?
(b) B 인도네시아 발리로 갔어요.
(c) A 좋은 시간 보내셨어요?
(d) B 물론이죠. 정말 재미있었어요.

PART IV **Identify the option that contains an awkward expression or an error in grammar.** (5문항)

문제유형 한 문단 속에 문법적으로 틀리거나 어색한 문장을 고르는 유형이다.

> (a) Morality is not the only reason for putting human rights on the West's foreign policy agenda. (b) Self-interest also plays a part in the process. (c) Political freedom tends to go hand in hand with economic freedom, which in turn tends to bring international trade and prosperity. (d) A world in which more countries respect basic human rights would be more peaceful place.

번역
(a) 서양의 외교정책 의제에 인권을 상정하는 유일한 이유가 도덕성은 아니다. (b) 자국의 이익 또한 그 과정에 일정 부분 관여한다. (c) 정치적 자유는 경제적 자유와 나란히 나아가는 경향이 있는데, 경제적 자유는 국제 무역과 번영을 가져오는 경향이 있다. (d) 더 많은 국가들이 기본적인 인권을 존중하는 세상은 더 평화로운 곳이 될 것이다.

Vocabulary 50문항

PART I

Choose the best answer for the blank. (25문항)

문제유형 A, B 대화 빈칸에 가장 적절한 단어를 넣는 유형이다. 단어의 단편적인 의미보다는 문맥에서 어떻게 쓰였는지 아는 것이 중요하다.

> A Let's take a coffee break.
> B I wish I could, but I'm _____ in work.

> ✔ (a) up to my eyeballs
> (b) green around the gills
> (c) against the grain
> (d) keeping my chin up

번역 A 잠깐 휴식 시간을 가집시다.
B 그러면 좋겠는데 일 때문에 꼼짝도 할 수가 없네요.

(a) ∼에 몰두하여
(b) 안색이 나빠 보이는
(c) 뜻이 맞지 않는
(d) 기운 내는

PART II

Choose the best answer for the blank. (25문항)

문제유형 문어체 문장의 빈칸에 가장 적절한 단어를 고르는 유형이다. 고난도 어휘의 독특한 용례를 따로 학습해 두어야 고득점이 가능하다.

> It takes a year for the earth to make one _____ around the sun.

(a) conversion
(b) circulation
(c) restoration
✔ (d) revolution

번역 지구가 태양 주위를 한 번 공전하는 데 일 년이 걸린다.
(a) 전환
(b) 순환
(c) 복구
(d) 공전

Reading Comprehension 40문항

Choose the option that best completes the passage. (16문항)

문제유형 지문의 논리적인 흐름을 파악하여 문맥상 빈칸에 가장 적절한 선택지를 고르는 문제이다.

> This product is a VCR-sized box that sits on or near a television and automatically records and stores television shows, sporting events and other TV programs, making them available for viewing later. This product lets users watch their favorite program _____. It's TV-on-demand that actually works, and no monthly fees.

    ✔ (a) whenever they want to
    (b) wherever they watch TV
    (c) whenever they are on TV
    (d) when the TV set is out of order

번역 이 제품은 텔레비전 옆에 놓인 VCR 크기의 상자로 TV 쇼, 스포츠 이벤트 및 다른 TV 프로그램을 자동으로 녹화 저장하여 나중에 볼 수 있게 해준다. 이 제품은 사용자가 자신이 가장 좋아하는 프로그램을 원하는 시간 언제나 볼 수 있게 해준다. 이것은 실제로 작동하는 주문형 TV로 매달 내는 시청료도 없다.

    (a) 원하는 시간 언제나
    (b) TV를 보는 곳 어디든지
    (c) TV에 나오는 언제나
    (d) TV가 작동되지 않을 때

Choose the option that best answers the question. (21문항)

문제유형 지문에 대한 이해를 측정하는 유형으로 주제 파악, 세부 내용 파악, 논리적 추론을 묻는 문제로 구성되어 있다.

> The pace of bank mergers is likely to accelerate. Recently Westbank has gained far more profit than it has lost through mergers, earning a record of $2.11 billion in 2003. Its shareholders have enjoyed an average gain of 28% a year over the past decade, beating the 18% annual return for the benchmark S&P stock index. However, when big banks get bigger, they have little interest in competing for those basic services many households prize. Consumers have to pay an average of 15% more a year, or $27.95, to maintain a regular checking account at a large bank instead of a smaller one.

    Q: What is the main topic of the passage?
    (a) Reasons for bank mergers
    ✔ (b) Effects of bank mergers
    (c) The merits of big banks
    (d) Increased profits of merged banks

번역 은행 합병 속도가 가속화될 전망이다. 최근 웨스트 뱅크가 2003년 21억 1천만 달러의 수익을 기록함으로써 합병으로 잃은 것보다 훨씬 더 많은 수익을 얻었다. 웨스트 뱅크 주주들은 지난 10년간 S&P 지수의 연간 수익률 18%를 웃도는 연평균 수익률 28%를 누려왔다. 하지만 규모가 더욱 커진 대형 은행들은 많은 가구가 중요하게 생각하는 기본 서비스에 대한 경쟁에는 별 관심을 두고 있지 않다. 소비자들은 작은 은행 대신 대형 은행의 보통 당좌예금 계정을 유지하기 위해 연평균 15% 이상, 즉 27달러 95센트를 지불해야 한다.

Q: 지문의 소재는?
(a) 은행 합병의 이유
(b) 은행 합병의 영향
(c) 대형 은행의 장점
(d) 합병된 은행들의 수익 증가

Identify the option that does NOT belong. (3문항)

문제유형 한 문단에서 전체의 흐름상 어색한 내용을 고르는 유형이다.

Communication with language is carried out through two basic human activities: speaking and listening. (a) These are of particular importance to psychologists, for they are mental activities that hold clues to the very nature of the human mind. (b) In speaking, people put ideas into words, talking about perceptions, feelings, and intentions they want other people to grasp. (c) In listening, people decode the sounds of words they hear to gain the intended meaning. (d) Language has stood at the center of human affairs throughout human history.

번역 언어로 이루어지는 의사소통은 두 가지 기본적인 인간 활동인 말하기와 듣기에 의해 수행된다. (a) 이 두 가지는 심리학자들에게 각별한 중요성을 지니는데, 이는 두 가지가 인간의 심성 본질 자체에 대한 단서를 쥐고 있는 정신적 활동이기 때문이다. (b) 말할 때 사람들은 다른 사람들이 이해하기를 원하는 지각과 감정, 의도 등을 말하면서 아이디어들을 단어로 표현한다. (c) 들을 때 사람들은 의도된 뜻을 간파하기 위해 들리는 단어의 소리를 해독한다. (d) 언어는 인류의 역사를 통틀어 인간 활동의 중심에 있어 왔다.

Actual Test 1

Listening Comprehension 💿
Grammar

Vocabulary

Reading Comprehension

LISTENING
COMPREHENSION

Part I **Questions 1—15**

You will now hear fifteen conversation fragments, each made up of a single spoken statement followed by four spoken responses. Choose the most appropriate response to the statement.

Part II **Questions 16—30**

You will now hear fifteen conversation fragments, each made up of three spoken statements followed by four spoken responses. Choose the most appropriate response to complete the conversation.

Part III **Questions 31—45**

You will now hear fifteen complete conversations. For each item, you will hear a conversation and its corresponding question, both of which will be read twice. Then you will hear four options which will be read only once. Choose the option that best answers the question.

Part IV **Questions 46—60**

You will now hear fifteen spoken monologues. For each item, you will hear a monologue and its corresponding question, both of which will be read twice. Then you will hear four options which will be read only once. Choose the option that best answers the question.

TEPS

GRAMMAR

DIRECTIONS

This part of the exam tests your grammar skills. You will have 25 minutes to complete the 50 questions. Be sure to follow the directions given by the proctor.

Part I **Questions 1—20**
Choose the best answer for the blank.

1. A: Do you exercise much?
    B: Yes, I go _____ in the park every afternoon.

    (a) jogging
    (b) to jogging
    (c) having jogged
    (d) to have jogged

2. A: I need to see Sylvia as soon as possible.
    B: Okay, I'll give her the message _____.

    (a) she arrives when
    (b) when she arrives
    (c) she will arrive when
    (d) when she will arrive

3. A: Hey there, Sam. How _____?
    B: Not great. I just got over a bad cold.

    (a) having been
    (b) do you have
    (c) have you been
    (d) are you having

4. A: I've got tickets to the symphony this Saturday.
    B: Really? What a coincidence! _____!

    (a) So do I
    (b) I do so
    (c) Do so I
    (d) So I do

5. A: Have you picked out a new computer for your office yet?
    B: No. I'm still _____ between the two top models.

    (a) decided
    (b) decisive
    (c) decision
    (d) deciding

6. A: Will you be able to finish the project by the deadline?
    B: Right now it looks that way, but I can't _____.

    (a) be sure
    (b) surely be
    (c) be sure of
    (d) have been sure

7. A: I can't wait for this weekend. Kim and Mike's wedding is going to be so much fun.
    B: I know. They _____ it for months!

    (a) plan
    (b) are planning
    (c) will be planning
    (d) have been planning

8. A: Okay, Ms. Johnson. Tell me about _____ biggest strengths.
    B: I have many strengths, but the most important one is that I'm a great team player.

    (a) your
    (b) yours
    (c) you're
    (d) you'll

9. A: Are you taking a vacation this summer?

   B: I enjoy _____, but I don't have the money for it right now.

   (a) to travel
   (b) traveling
   (c) the traveling
   (d) being traveled

10. A: _____ down the music just a little? I'm trying to get some sleep.

    B: Of course not. I didn't realize it was so loud.

    (a) Mind your turning
    (b) Would you mind turning
    (c) You mind having turned
    (d) Wouldn't you have turned

11. A: My name is Henry Dawson and I'd like to check in now.

    B: Okay, Mr. Dawson. Your room will _____ in five minutes.

    (a) be ready
    (b) be already
    (c) have been readily
    (d) have been already

12. A: Do you know what you're going to write about for your essay?

    B: I've thought long and hard, but I still _____.

    (a) no idea have
    (b) have no idea
    (c) an idea haven't
    (d) haven't had idea

13. A: I wasn't going to vote in the election, but my wife convinced me to.

    B: I knew she _____.

    (a) would
    (b) would do
    (c) would have to do
    (d) would have that

14. A: How can you be sure that your lawyer _____ the plaintiff's?

    B: Well, he graduated at the top of his class from Harvard Law.

    (a) knows more
    (b) has more knowledge
    (c) has been knowing more than
    (d) is more knowledgeable than

15. A: Professor, I'm not sure _____ I understand the science project.

    B: Let's go over it again, shall we?

    (a) if
    (b) as
    (c) like
    (d) what

16. A: I'm afraid the new supervisor won't be able to improve work performance.

    B: All he has to do is raise our output _____.

    (a) less
    (b) least
    (c) little
    (d) a little

17. A: Kathy and Anna seem very close.
       They spend practically all their
       time together.
    B: Yes, they've known _____
       since grade school.

    (a) others
    (b) another
    (c) one other
    (d) each other

18. A: I can't believe someone lost the
       client list.
    B: _____ did is in a lot of
       trouble.

    (a) Whoever
    (b) Whatever
    (c) Whichever
    (d) Whenever

19. A: This store is terrible. I've been
       here for hours and I haven't found
       _____ jacket in my size.
    B: I told you, you should have tried
       the one in the mall.

    (a) the
    (b) any
    (c) this
    (d) each

20. A: Have you heard? Mr. Martinez is
       being released from the hospital
       today.
    B: _____ he passes his final
       blood test, that is.

    (a) Assume
    (b) Assumed
    (c) Assuming
    (d) To assume

Part II **Questions 21—40**

Choose the best answer for the blank.

---

21. Jimmy had trouble _____ all
    the dishes while the dishwasher was
    broken.

    (a) wash
    (b) to wash
    (c) washed
    (d) washing

22. The style of art _____
    Impressionism was created in the
    1860s by a group of French painters.

    (a) known as
    (b) to know as
    (c) like knowing
    (d) to be known

23. _____ all night for a test can
    actually lead to less retention of
    knowledge in the long run.

    (a) Studied
    (b) Studying
    (c) He studied
    (d) As he studied

24. Geoffrey Chaucer was the first major
    author _____ literary works in
    the English language, as opposed to
    Latin or French.

    (a) wrote
    (b) to write
    (c) in writing
    (d) had written

25. Despite what the commercial said, Katie doubted that _____ could really help improve her time in the 400 meters.

(a) pairs of shoe
(b) a pair of shoe
(c) pairs of shoes
(d) a pair of shoes

26. Some people _____ in order to lose a little weight.

(a) an extremely measured
(b) go to extreme measures
(c) measure extremely to go
(d) went to measure an extreme

27. Pluto is now classified as a Kuiper Belt Object, whereas it _____ considered one of the solar system's planets.

(a) uses to
(b) is to use
(c) was of use
(d) used to be

28. The newspaper's music critic published _____ review of my band's performance that I didn't play guitar for a week.

(a) such bad
(b) a bad such
(c) a such bad
(d) such a bad

29. The sea otter is _____ animals that uses tools to prepare its food.

(a) of only a few
(b) a few of the one
(c) only a few of one
(d) one of only a few

30. For seven years, Jason has worked _____ a chef at one of New York's most popular restaurants.

(a) as
(b) on
(c) at
(d) in

31. The professor informed everyone that behavior in the classroom that disrupts the learning of other students will _____.

(a) not tolerate
(b) be not tolerate
(c) not be tolerated
(d) be not tolerated

32. Business travelers are advised to take a course on _____ of their destination prior to embarking.

(a) custom
(b) few customs
(c) some custom
(d) the customs

33. The members of the school board _____ William as a gifted and promising student.

(a) thought of always
(b) always was thinking
(c) had thoughts of always
(d) have always thought of

34. The thief was caught while _____ into another jewelry store last night.

(a) break
(b) broken
(c) breaks
(d) breaking

35. Samuel bought a new digital camera and asked Conrad to show him _____.

    (a) how to use it
    (b) to how it use
    (c) using it how
    (d) how it used to

36. Health experts maintain that _____ more than two cups of coffee a day.

    (a) you drink ought to
    (b) drinking you ought
    (c) you ought not to drink
    (d) ought not your drinking

37. Local tourism agencies recommend _____ the rare animals in the city zoo.

    (a) to visitors see of
    (b) that visitors see
    (c) visitors see that
    (d) seeing the visitors

38. _____ interested in learning more about the history of the California Gold Rush can find information on the library's website.

    (a) They
    (b) Every
    (c) Them
    (d) Anyone

39. Most parents agree that raising children is _____ thing they've ever done.

    (a) most rewarded
    (b) a most rewarded
    (c) mostly rewarding
    (d) the most rewarding

40. No one knows what _____ have happened if the United States had fought on the side of the Germans in World War I.

    (a) will
    (b) must
    (c) should
    (d) would

Part III **Questions 41—45**

Identify the option that contains an awkward expression or an error in grammar.

41. (a) A: You always do so well in science class.
    (b) B: Well, it's a lot the more enjoyable for me than other subjects.
    (c) A: Do you think you could help me study for our test next week?
    (d) B: Of course. I'd be happy to help you out.

42. (a) A: Have you seen Robert? How'd his interview go?
    (b) B: Excellent. He was naming the new head of sales.
    (c) A: That's terrific! He must be thrilled.
    (d) B: He is. And the company's excited to have him.

43. (a) A: Sir, I'm afraid your reservation was accidentally canceled.
    (b) B: Really? Are there any other rooms available?
    (c) A: Yes. I've booked you into a double instead of a single, and sorry for the inconvenience.
    (d) B: Don't worry about it. All we make mistakes.

44. (a) A: Dr. Carter is with another patient, so your appointment will be delayed.
    (b) B: That's unfortunate. Do you know how long he'll be?
    (c) A: He shouldn't be long. You can wait right over there.
    (d) B: Well, I hope he can see me until 5:00 because I have another engagement at 5:30.

45. (a) A: I have a lot of studying to do in the library today.
    (b) B: Me, too. There's a major test I need to prepare for.
    (c) A: Is that so? Who's class is it for?
    (d) B: Professor Donovan. Her exams are always incredibly difficult.

Part IV Questions 46—50

Identify the option that contains an awkward expression or an error in grammar.

46. (a) It's understandable that some people object to scientific research harms animals. (b) But the truth is that this kind of experimentation has many benefits. (c) Animal testing allows scientists to develop new drugs that can cure serious human diseases. (d) If it weren't for animal research, we wouldn't have developed penicillin, which is now used to treat many ailments.

47. (a) Grease residue can remain on your pots and pans for years, ruining the taste of everything you cook. (b) To eliminate grease, it's time you added a new weapon to your kitchen: Grease Buster. (c) Grease Buster's patented cleansing formula has been showing to remove twice as much residue as leading brands of dish soap. (d) You won't be able to recognize your old pots and pans after one application of Grease Buster—guaranteed.

48. (a) The Arc de Triomphe is one of the most iconic structures in Paris. (b) It was designed in 1806, but the construction work was not completed until the 1830s. (c) Based on a classical Roman design, it is nearly 30 meters tall and 15 meters in width. (d) The enormous arch honors France's soldiers and the generals who led themselves into battle.

49. (a) Before the nineteenth century, every city or region kept its own time, based on the occurrence of local noon. (b) However, with the advent of railroads, the lack of a standardized time system became a problem. (c) People were now able to travel long distances very quickly, so to avoid confusion it was necessary for different locales to keep the same time. (d) By the end of the century, most countries have adopted the worldwide time standard we use today.

50. (a) Most students who attend university has experienced an "all-nighter," where they stay up all night studying for a big exam. (b) Yet studies show that this method of studying is not very effective. (c) When we're tired, our minds are unable to retain information in any sort of meaningful way. (d) In other words, you may be able to pass your test after pulling an all-nighter, but you're unlikely to remember the information in the long term.

This is the end of the Grammar section. Do NOT move on to the next section until instructed to do so. You are NOT allowed to turn to any other section of the test.

VOCABULARY

Part I **Questions 1—25**

Choose the best answer for the blank.

1. A: Thanks for buying dinner. I'll leave the _____.
    B: No, it was included in the bill.

    (a) tip
    (b) gift
    (c) check
    (d) change

2. A: We missed you at the movie yesterday.
    B: Sorry I couldn't make it. My car got a _____ on the way there.

    (a) tire
    (b) flat
    (c) spare
    (d) wheel

3. A: Can I give you a(n) _____ to finish any of these reports?
    B: Thanks, but I should be able to manage.

    (a) run
    (b) offer
    (c) hand
    (d) chance

4. A: I didn't really understand the plot of the book.
    B: Don't worry. I can _____ for you.

    (a) sum it up
    (b) tell it off
    (c) turn it on
    (d) leave it out

5. A: Can you believe I only paid $10 for this cell phone?
    B: What a _____!

    (a) steal
    (b) thief
    (c) crime
    (d) robbery

6. A: I'm worried I'm going to fail my calculus class.
    B: If you need extra help, I know a great _____.

    (a) tutor
    (b) mentor
    (c) advertiser
    (d) professor

7. A: Could you _____ me a few sheets of paper? I left my notebook at home.
    B: I only have one piece, and I need it for myself.

    (a) pay
    (b) lend
    (c) provide
    (d) borrow

8. A: Where are we going to _____ the football game tomorrow?
    B: How about my house?

    (a) eye
    (b) look
    (c) sight
    (d) watch

9. A: Don't forget your jacket when you leave today. It's freezing out there.
   B: You're right. I wouldn't want to _____ a cold.
   (a) find
   (b) grab
   (c) catch
   (d) keep

10. A: I didn't enjoy the taste of that new chicken recipe.
    B: Neither did I. I could _____ eat mine.
    (a) hardly
    (b) surely
    (c) poorly
    (d) finally

11. A: Is there someone who can help me _____ my groceries?
    B: I can do that. Would you like paper or plastic?
    (a) bag
    (b) fill
    (c) sack
    (d) case

12. A: I'm afraid Professor Robinson isn't in his office right now.
    B: That's okay. I'll _____ later.
    (a) take back
    (b) hang out
    (c) carry out
    (d) check back

13. A: The words in this poem really paints a picture, don't they?
    B: Yes, the _____ is beautiful.
    (a) imagery
    (b) erosion
    (c) strokes
    (d) fracture

14. A: Are you thinking about buying a new air conditioner?
    B: Yes, but I'll probably _____ until winter, when prices are lower.
    (a) lift up
    (b) hold off
    (c) move on
    (d) figure out

15. A: It looks like Park Drive is closed up ahead due to construction.
    B: We'll have to make a _____ around the park, I guess.
    (a) path
    (b) route
    (c) detour
    (d) highway

16. A: I just heard the defendant cut a deal, so we won't have to _____ the case.
    B: That's good news. Our evidence was pretty thin, anyway.
    (a) dilute
    (b) attribute
    (c) prosecute
    (d) substitute

17. A: How much _____ do hotels charge in this country?
    B: It's around fifteen percent, I believe.
    (a) tax
    (b) fee
    (c) pay
    (d) cost

18. A: This used coat would look great on me.

B: Check it closely before you buy it. This store doesn't accept _____.

(a) refunds
(b) returns
(c) rebates
(d) receipts

19. A: Make sure not to _____ any sensitive information during the convention.

B: Right. I wouldn't want to help out any of our competitors.

(a) coerce
(b) exempt
(c) sanction
(d) disclose

20. A: I pleaded with Jon not to sell his house in such a buyer's market, but he didn't listen.

B: I know. His decision doesn't _____ well with me, either.

(a) sit
(b) feel
(c) stay
(d) seem

21. A: What do you think of the new intern?

B: She's brilliant. Her contribution to the budget plan was _____.

(a) invaluable
(b) ostentatious
(c) substandard
(d) theoretical

22. A: Why should I talk with a trainer at the gym?

B: He can help you develop a fitness _____ that works for you.

(a) sojourn
(b) regimen
(c) appraisal
(d) rendition

23. A: Gas is so expensive these days.

B: I know it. I'm paying close to $100 every time I _____!

(a) fill up
(b) buy out
(c) pump out
(d) pull down

24. A: I'm sorry we couldn't agree on which sofa to buy.

B: Don't apologize. It's I who should be taking the _____.

(a) fault
(b) turn
(c) guilt
(d) blame

25. A: What do you consider when you _____ your monthly budget?

B: Everything from bills to spending for entertainment.

(a) add
(b) count
(c) figure
(d) number

Choose the best answer for the blank.

26. Yuri Gagarin, the Soviet cosmonaut, became the first man to _____ into space on April 12, 1961.

    (a) exhale
    (b) repulse
    (c) venture
    (d) convene

27. During the Middle Ages in Europe, noblemen who owned land were given the _____ of baron.

    (a) title
    (b) calling
    (c) address
    (d) caricature

28. The singer's fans were upset that she canceled the concert without any _____ warning.

    (a) prior
    (b) adjacent
    (c) former
    (d) rabid

29. Each customer who _____ us feedback about the new promotion will be entered into a drawing to win a new stereo.

    (a) gives
    (b) grants
    (c) allows
    (d) retrieves

30. Politicians have no _____ for their errors to become public knowledge.

    (a) will
    (b) care
    (c) idea
    (d) desire

31. Due to the tremendous rate of _____, the price of bread rose by nearly 50% overnight.

    (a) tariff
    (b) inflation
    (c) downturn
    (d) commission

32. The famous novelist gets most of the _____ material for his books from his real-life travels through the Middle East.

    (a) raw
    (b) gruff
    (c) barren
    (d) meager

33. People of the Rifard region have a bad reputation for rudeness among tourists but some are quite _____.

    (a) habitual
    (b) indisposed
    (c) impetuous
    (d) hospitable

34. Scientists are nearly finished designing an advanced telescope to send into _____ around the Earth.

    (a) orbit
    (b) circuit
    (c) distance
    (d) revolution

35. Most children these days are allowed too much freedom for their own

    _____.

    (a) good
    (b) brevity
    (c) wealth
    (d) reason

36. It is easy to _____ the entire dish by adding too much salt or pepper.

    (a) ruin
    (b) crash
    (c) delude
    (d) damage

37. The environmental organization charges that the tire manufacturer acted _____ when it decided to dump its chemical waste in the river.

    (a) blatantly
    (b) concisely
    (c) pertinently
    (d) negligently

38. Michael's Seafood is best known for its lobster plate, which _____ with a salad, a side of vegetables, and fries.

    (a) stays
    (b) joins
    (c) tables
    (d) comes

39. These days, in order to _____ a good job you really need to have a graduate degree.

    (a) land
    (b) swipe
    (c) discover
    (d) inflate

40. The doctor _____ his patient a mild sedative to treat her insomnia.

    (a) donated
    (b) extended
    (c) prescribed
    (d) transmitted

41. The company gave the workers one week to review the labor _____ and either sign it or submit their proposed revisions.

    (a) script
    (b) record
    (c) contract
    (d) evidence

42. World War I textbooks often label the powers of the Triple Alliance as the _____, but the truth is that neither side was completely blameless.

    (a) treaties
    (b) armistices
    (c) detonators
    (d) aggressors

43. Due to a need for more productivity, company employees will no longer be allowed to take _____ in the afternoons.

    (a) lapses
    (b) breaks
    (c) intervals
    (d) stoppages

44. Sign language was developed in the 18th century to _____ communication with deaf people and is now widely used.

(a) nullify
(b) convolute
(c) endorse
(d) facilitate

45. The company recently accused of financial fraud has learned that a government task force is planning to _____ its yearly records.

(a) audit
(b) contort
(c) gauge
(d) balance

46. The Pope is the most important figure in Catholicism and is _____ with directing Catholic doctrine worldwide.

(a) sworn
(b) upheld
(c) charged
(d) positioned

47. Artificial pesticides are one of the primary substances that are _____ our rivers.

(a) littering
(b) polluting
(c) irrigating
(d) weakening

48. The accounting software that was released yesterday already has over 10,000 registered _____.

(a) users
(b) shoppers
(c) employees
(d) technicians

49. The employee's promotion is being postponed until _____ of misconduct can be investigated.

(a) situations
(b) royalties
(c) allegations
(d) formalities

50. All medical research must involve both a control group and an experimental group if its findings are to be _____.

(a) contrived
(b) appeased
(c) expunged
(d) legitimized

This is the end of the Vocabulary section. Do NOT move on to the Reading Comprehension section until instructed to do so. You are NOT allowed to turn to any other section of the test.

READING
COMPREHENSION

Part I **Questions 1—16**

Read the passage. Then choose the option that best completes the passage.

---

1. You know it's true, even though you may not want to admit it: you don't get enough exercise. National health statistics show that nearly 30% of the population suffers from obesity. At the same time, it's been proven that even modest amounts of exercise can reduce one's risk of obesity-related diseases. You don't have to turn yourself into an athletic superstar or a 300-pound bodybuilder to _____.
Join Pat's Gym today and we'll show you exactly what it takes to create a better you.

   (a) gain that extra muscle
   (b) achieve a healthy level of fitness
   (c) become more active in these sports
   (d) recover from a life-threatening illness

2. The creation of virtual online worlds is a troubling trend. Games and programs that encourage users to construct entire existences apart from their lives in the real world are dangerous to our way of life. They prevent our youth from learning valuable social skills and make it too easy for others to ignore their responsibilities. If everyone spends their time in artificial worlds, _____.

   (a) the gaming industry will boom
   (b) their skills will greatly improve
   (c) the real one may cease to function
   (d) they might understand young people better

3. Scientists aren't exactly sure why moths tend to fly towards light bulbs and candle flames, which is sometimes a fatal behavior. One theory ties it to the _____. In natural dark skies, moths may rely on the distant light of the moon to find their way. Man-made artificial light sources confuse the insects, causing them to constantly adjust their flight patterns to coordinate with the bright light they assume is the moon. Many wind up getting too close and burning their delicate bodies and wings.

   (a) heat given off by bright lights
   (b) odd shape of the insect's wings
   (c) process they use for navigation
   (d) poor night vision of these creatures

4. Banner ads and popup windows _____. Research shows they have been losing their effectiveness as users become more and more familiar with them. Companies interested in utilizing the next wave of Internet marketing are embracing content-based marketing. Through this method, ad material is embedded directly into the text of popular websites, much like the product placement techniques seen in movies.

(a) will soon be undergoing a transformation
(b) are reliable sources of advertising revenue
(c) attract web surfers from different demographics
(d) represent traditional forms of online advertising

5. Modern professional duties have become increasingly location-independent, even for corporate executives. It can be difficult to hold meetings when you have 15 different executives in 15 different locales. Thankfully, this problem is solved in large part by videoconferencing. Through a combination of video and audio technologies, it allows face-to-face, real-time interaction among agents who physically may be thousands of miles apart. Videoconferencing, therefore, is the preferred medium of communication for _____.

(a) employees of telecommunications firms
(b) traveling salespeople seeking new contacts
(c) corporations with a multinational presence
(d) executives who have a demanding work schedule

6. Mary Shelley's 1818 debut novel Frankenstein is significant in many respects. In it, she pioneered the use of a plot structure that creates a framework around the main action. Instead of directly relating the plot herself, it is a character within the novel that tells the story secondhand through a letter. Moreover, Frankenstein is seen by many today as the first true science-fiction novel. Its mix of science, fantasy, and horror was more or less unique for the time. Therefore, Shelley's novel is recognized as groundbreaking _____.

(a) in both stylistic and thematic contexts
(b) for influencing so many female authors
(c) despite its use of secondhand storytelling
(d) because of its inclusion of intellectual subjects

7. Is your idea of a good time standing knee-deep in an ice-cold stream, reeling in a 20-inch rainbow trout? If your answer is "Yes," then a subscription to Fly Fishing Monthly is just what you need. Sign up today and we'll send you 18 issues of this award-winning magazine for the incredible low price of $25.99. That's a savings of over $30 off the list price! Moreover, you'll be getting the best coverage available on _____.

    (a) all water-related outdoor activities
    (b) everything related to the world of fly fishing
    (c) deals being offered in the publishing industry
    (d) health updates regarding the consumption of fish

8. Throughout the seventeenth to nineteenth centuries, the exchange of goods in the West was dominated by the Transatlantic Triangular Trade. As in any form of triangular trade, _____. In Africa, people were captured and shipped to the Americas as slaves. There, their labor was utilized to produce raw goods such as cotton, sugar, and tobacco. These were in turn shipped to England, where manufacturers processed them into products that were sold in Africa and elsewhere in the world.

    (a) there were three principal regions involved
    (b) one partner was more powerful than the others
    (c) the products being shipped were agricultural in nature
    (d) the human rights of those involved were not recognized

9.

Dear customer service representative,

I am writing in regards to a refurbished EasyScan 600 portable scanner that I purchased from your company on August 6. According to the certificate of refurbishment I received with the product, its condition had been completely restored and it was guaranteed to function as well as a brand-new EasyScan 600. However, after only one week of use, the rollers that feed paper through the scanning device stopped working. _____, I am unable to operate the scanner and am requesting a full refund.

Sincerely,
Eileen Chambers

(a) Without a replacement part
(b) Until the problem is resolved
(c) Despite the rollers' malfunction
(d) As a result of this product defect

10. Modern surfers owe a debt to one man: Duke Kahanamoku. Though surfing was an ancient tradition among the Hawaiian people, Kahanamoku is credited with popularizing it throughout the world. He traveled extensively, giving exhibitions of the sport in addition to his tremendous swimming talents. He brought the fad to California in 1914, and to this day the state is known as a hotbed of surfing culture. _____, he is now immortalized in legend among surfers everywhere.

(a) Because of his latest win
(b) Due to his unique surfing style
(c) For his contributions to the sport
(d) In spite of his controversial reputation

11. Beginning in the early 1900s, psychologists came to believe that birth order played an important role in a child's psychological development. That is, when a child was born in relation to his or her siblings had strong implications for his or her mental characteristics. The theory held that firstborn children demonstrated greater independence and social dominance, whereas later-borns tended to be more agreeable and open to compromise. In recent years, however, many have dismissed this theory, arguing that birth order _____.

(a) is part of our genetic makeup
(b) has little or no effect on personality
(c) is more important than parental care
(d) has become irrelevant in these species

12. In Greek mythology, the nine Muses were goddesses responsible for imparting creativity to humanity. Poets, storytellers, musicians, and playwrights all acknowledged the Muses for endowing their work with wisdom and meaning. According to myth, they were daughters of Zeus, king of the gods, and led by Apollo, the god of the arts. The Muses remain a part of our culture today, fulfilling a very similar role. For example, we still use the word "muse" to name _____.

    (a) our motivation for creating art
    (b) an artist whose work we bought
    (c) a mysterious occurrence we don't understand
    (d) the inspiration behind our creative endeavors

13. Tom Michaels _____. As a teenager, he started a small company transporting documents and packages for local businesspeople on his bicycle. He continued with this enterprise throughout his school years. After graduation, he was ready to expand. He hired 20 cyclists to carry out deliveries around the city. Soon, he was earning enough money to add a handful of trucks to his fleet. The rest is history: Michaels went on to build the most successful shipping company on the planet.

    (a) inherited his family's shipping business
    (b) is a major advocate for the use of bicycles
    (c) has been in the delivery business all his life
    (d) experienced both ups and downs in his life

14. Scholars often point to an English legal charter drafted in the year 1215 as the earliest sign of democracy in Western Europe. Known by its Latin name, Magna Carta, its purpose was to force King John to guarantee certain rights to his subjects. In essence, it was the first time an English king had admitted to being bound by the rule of law. Though a far cry from the guiding documents of modern governments, it nonetheless represents an important steppingstone in _____.

    (a) the rise of individual self-expression
    (b) a shift towards greater English power
    (c) the evolution of today's democratic nation-states
    (d) a movement to abolish the monarchy in England

15. In many ecosystems, there is often a single species—most typically an animal species—whose existence is vital to ensuring a healthy balance within the ecosystem. Such species are known as keystone species. Much like the keystone that forms the apex of an arch, the keystone species maintains the structure and order of natural processes among the other members of its habitat. It may do so in a number of ways. _____, the predation of a keystone species may control the populations of other species that would otherwise explode and overwhelm the ecosystem.

   (a) Regardlessly
   (b) For instance
   (c) At the same time
   (d) Despite this fact

16. Along with the rise of the automobile in America came that of drive-in theaters, outdoor facilities where movies were projected to be viewed by people in their cars. The popularity of drive-ins peaked in the 1950s and '60s. They appealed to teenagers, who saw it as a great opportunity to escape their parents and go on dates. _____, families with young children enjoyed being able to bring their kids to the movies without having to worry about them disturbing other members of the audience. The '70s saw a decline in drive-ins, but in recent years there have been nostalgic revivals across the country.

   (a) Hereby
   (b) Likewise
   (c) Consequently
   (d) On the contrary

Read the passage and the question. Then choose the option that best answers the question.

17. Researchers have handed smokers yet another reason to kick the habit: third-hand smoke. For years, we've heard reports of how secondhand smoke, that which is inhaled by people standing close to smokers, can negatively affect our health. As it turns out, though, cigarettes produce toxins that linger long after the smoke has dissipated. A study carried out by Mass General Hospital for Children found that toxic particulates present in cigarette smoke cling to clothing, hair, and other objects and can later be ingested and cause harm, especially to children.

Q: What is the main idea of the passage?

(a) Cigarettes harm with more than smoke.
(b) Smoking should be prohibited in homes.
(c) Children are particularly vulnerable to tobacco smoke.
(d) Third-hand smoke is more dangerous than secondhand smoke.

18. At National Airways, we know you're fed up with all the extra fees being charged by airlines these days. That's why we're happy to introduce "1 Bag Free." On every National Airways flight, you'll be able to check one luggage item free of charge, no matter how short the journey. This is a big improvement over other carriers who continue to charge high fees for your first checked bag.

Q: What is mainly being advertised?

(a) A limited-time deal on airfare
(b) An airline's new baggage policy
(c) A new method for checking bags
(d) A recently created budget air carrier

19. One of the earliest and most important works of English literature is the epic poem *Beowulf*. Although written in Old English, which differs significantly from the modern language, *Beowulf*'s influence can be seen in the works of countless English-language authors. It tells the story of an Anglo-Saxon warrior who battles different monsters in order to keep his people safe. As such, the character of *Beowulf* can also be seen as the culture's first hero.

Q: What is the best title for the passage?

(a) Reinterpreting the Meaning of *Beowulf*
(b) Appearances of Heroes in English Literature
(c) Examining the Old English Used in *Beowulf*
(d) Background to the Significance of *Beowulf*

20. Spring City's 180th anniversary celebration promises to be a lot of fun. As always, there's something for the whole family. Kids will love the custom-built inflatable castle and swimming pool, while adults can kick back and listen to the melodious tunes of Spring City's own Rockin' Jukebox Band. Please note that the event will not be held on August 5 this year, but instead will take place on Saturday, August 3. This should ensure a great turnout, so don't miss it!

Q: What is the announcement mainly about?

(a) Scheduling and activity details for a local festival
(b) Safety information concerning children's fair activities
(c) The postponement of an annual community celebration
(d) An upcoming rock-and-roll concert taking place in town

21. When Ricardo Diaz opened the not-for-profit Bread and Butter Bureau years ago, all he knew was that he wanted to help deliver food to homeless people in the Los Angeles area. Little did he know that six short years later he'd be leading an operation that had become a leader in California's homeless rights movement. The BBB was quick to score several large private donations from LA philanthropists, which is what enabled its rapid expansion. But if you talk to Diaz today, you'll encounter the same intensity and passion for his cause that he possessed six years ago.

Q: What is the passage mainly about?

(a) An ex-homeless business entrepreneur
(b) A nonprofit success story in California
(c) The business model of a charitable group
(d) The plight of the homeless in Los Angeles

22. Today, film posters are collectors' hot items, but it wasn't always so. In the golden age of film, the 1940s and '50s, posters were produced in small quantities by film distribution companies and leaned to theaters on a temporary basis. Under this system, posters seldom found their way to the general public. Things didn't change until the 1980s, when recording studios took over the responsibility of creating posters and started mass-producing them. Consequently, posters advertising films from the '70s and earlier can be rare and incredibly valuable.

Q: What is the best title for the passage?
(a) Movie Posters during Film's Golden Age
(b) The Evolution of the Art of Film Posters
(c) The History behind Movie Poster Distribution
(d) Why People Enjoy Collecting Hollywood Posters

23. Robert LeRoy Parker, better known as Butch Cassidy, is one of the Wild West's most infamous figures. What many people don't realize, though, is that Parker spent the last eight years of his life not in Colorado or New Mexico, but rather in South America. To escape criminal charges in the U.S., he fled to Argentina in 1901. His initial intention was to lead a new, law-abiding life. However, he soon returned to robbery to earn a living and was killed by Bolivian army troops in 1908.

Q: Which of the following is correct about Parker according to the passage?
(a) He became a lawman in Argentina.
(b) He was born and raised in Colorado.
(c) He was an outlaw in America's Wild West.
(d) He was wrongly accused of robbery in Bolivia.

24. The sport of soccer is popularly termed "the world's game," and rightly so. Many countries attempt to claim credit for the invention of soccer. While the majority of rules governing the modern version of the game come from England, similar sports were played throughout history by different cultures. FIFA, the official international body in charge of determining soccer policy, points to the ancient Chinese game of cuju as the first known incarnation.

Q: Which of the following is correct according to the passage?
(a) There is no single origin of the soccer.
(b) The sport of soccer has multiple governing organizations.
(c) The Chinese invented many of the rules for the modern soccer.
(d) Today's soccer is played differently in England than it is elsewhere.

25. The popularity of Nashville country music in the early 1960s produced many revered stars, and Patsy Cline was one of the most memorable. Her melodic voice ensured that songs like "I Fall to Pieces" and "Crazy" became unstoppable hits. Unfortunately, the singer seemed to be destined for disaster. She suffered two serious automobile accidents, the second of which nearly took her life. Then, in 1963, Cline's plane crashed while en route to Nashville, killing everyone on board. She was only 30 years old.

Q: Which of the following is correct according to the passage?
(a) Cline often traveled by plane.
(b) Nashville was Cline's birthplace.
(c) Cline wrote only two popular songs.
(d) Cline came close to dying in a car crash.

26. Sudden infant death syndrome (SIDS) remains one of the biggest mysteries in early-life healthcare. Infants perishing from SIDS are found dead in their cribs after being put to bed. They show no symptoms of illness before the onset of SIDS, and autopsies reveal no definitive cause of death. Though the mechanism that triggers SIDS is still unknown, many health professionals feel that a child's risk can be minimized by putting him or her to sleep in a supine, or face-up, position. This comes on the heels of numerous studies suggesting that babies set in their cribs in the prone (face-down) position are more likely to die from SIDS.

Q: Which of the following is correct according to the passage?
(a) The cause of SIDS is related to the infant's sleep position.
(b) It's possible to manage the risk but not prevent SIDS altogether.
(c) Traditional child autopsies do not investigate the cause of SIDS.
(d) Children who sleep supinely are healthier than those sleeping in the prone position.

27. From the ninth to the nineteenth centuries A.D., southern and central Vietnam was controlled by the Champa kingdom. The Cham people were seafarers who spoke a language related to Malay and practiced the religion of Hinduism. Though its existence lasted for many centuries, Champa was constantly threatened by its neighbors. To the north lay Dai Viet, home of the predecessors of today's Vietnamese, and to the west was the vast Khmer empire. These three powers warred and traded territory back and forth for hundreds of years, but in the end Champa proved incapable of resisting two simultaneous pressures.

Q: Which of the following is correct according to the passage?
(a) Champa's dependence on the ocean proved to be a weakness.
(b) The religion of Champa was different from that of the Khmer.
(c) Champa was more powerful than Dai Viet before the ninth century.
(d) The Cham are not considered forerunners of the modern Vietnamese.

28. The authority and reputation of the Catholic Church has been shaken recently by a series of sexual abuse cases brought against priests. Most of the earliest reported cases occurred in the Boston archdiocese, and most involved the abuse of minors. Later, the courage of victims there prompted others around the country and the world to come forward with their own stories and allegations. Most shocking is the fact that the Church seems to have known about the priests' actions. However, instead of punishing them, authorities simply transferred the priests to other parishes.

Q: Which of the following is correct according to the passage?
(a) Boston saw few of the sexual abuse cases.
(b) The offending priests have recently been punished.
(c) The majority of victims of abuse were young people.
(d) Catholic parishes around the world have expressed regret.

29. Claude Monet is seen as the most important founding member of the artistic school of Impressionism. Indeed, it was his painting Impression, Sunrise from which the style took its name in 1870s France. Central to Monet's artistic philosophy was a dismissal of the past and a reliance on his own subjective experience of the world. It was a revolutionary approach, but one the international art community came to identify with strongly. Monet is still widely popular in the twenty-first century. His work regularly sells for over $20 million.

Q: Which of the following is correct about Monet according to the passage?

(a) His art is in high demand today.
(b) His style was copied by many painters.
(c) He received no formal training in painting.
(d) He named a painting after his art movement.

30.

Dear Mr. Hank Hensley

The Windy Beach Condominium Complex will soon be undergoing some much-needed renovations that may affect the supply of certain utilities to your unit. From August 29 to October 10, the complex's sewer system will be completely overhauled. In order to allow the work to proceed, the water main will occasionally be turned off, blocking transmission of potable water to all units in your building. We recommend stocking up on bottled water so you are not inconvenienced during the outages.

Thank you for your cooperation,
Windy Beach Condominium Owners Board

Q: Which of the following is correct according to the letter?

(a) It is advisable that Mr. Hensley buys his own water.
(b) The maintenance work will last for several months.
(c) The interior of Mr. Hensley's unit will be renovated.
(d) Mr. Hensley will experience periodic power outages.

31. The 2009 swine flu pandemic was a rare case in which a virus causing influenza in pigs also created a contagious illness in humans. Ordinarily, strains of the swine influenza virus may pass from pigs to humans, but it cannot be transferred from human to human. The last major occurrence of human spread flu came in 1918 during a major flu outbreak. Research has shown that swine influenza viruses are always present in pigs, but that it is only when they mutate in certain ways that they pose a threat to humans.

Q: Which of the following is correct according to the passage?

(a) The swine influenza virus first appeared in 1918.
(b) Swine flu is usually transmittable between humans.
(c) The recent swine flu outbreak represents an anomaly.
(d) Swine and human influenzas are virtually indistinguishable.

32. We may like to believe that parents care for each of their children equally. But recent research done by the Institute of Evolutionary Science shows that fathers give more care to children that resemble them physically. The study involved thirty families in several villages in Senegal. For each father-child pair, measurements were taken of how closely the child resembled the father and how much time he spent with the child. The results suggest that the more a child looks like its father, the more time he will invest in the child's growth and development.

Q: Which of the following is correct according to the passage?
(a) The study took into account two variables.
(b) Fathers in Senegal are more caring than others.
(c) Childcare is influenced by the gender of the child.
(d) A father's care is essential to a child's development.

33.

Dear Editor:

Last Thursday, I read an article in your paper discussing the questionable impact of charitable donations. The author, Lynn Smith, suggested that it's impossible to know if your charity dollars are being spent appropriately. As the national director of the organization Options for Orphans, I was deeply offended by this article. At Options for Orphans, 80% of the donations we receive go directly to orphans around the world. We also report on our finances twice annually, so contributors can see where their money is going. I would very much like to see a letter of apology for Ms. Smith's misinformed and irresponsible article.

Q: What can be inferred from the letter?
(a) Lynn Smith runs a charitable operation.
(b) The writer will publish a letter of rebuttal.
(c) Options for Orphans is a new organization.
(d) Options for Orphans strives to be accountable.

34. Vertical integration refers to a business model in which a single entity controls all steps in the production, promotion, and distribution of a product. The phrase famously came into being to describe the Carnegie Steel company. Carnegie owned the iron mines, the ships that transported the iron ore, the steel processing facilities, and even the railroads that delivered the final product. While vertical integration can generate impressive profits for companies, it also has its problems. For example, vertically integrated operations often wind up dominating the market as monopolies, and it is consumers who suffer.

Q: What can be inferred from the passage?
(a) Vertical integration is a threat to consumers rights.
(b) Consumers rarely voice concerns about vertical integration.
(c) Vertical integration delivers guaranteed product quality.
(d) Many of today's companies choose to adopt vertical integration.

35. The theory of emotional memory in psychology holds that events accompanied by strong emotions lead to the creation of clearer, longer-lasting memories. But exactly how long the details of a memory last also depends on the hue of the emotion. For example, among the general population, events that generate positive emotions are remembered more powerfully than those that cause negative emotions. The average person is also more likely to recall a positive memory at any given moment. This dynamic reverses, however, in people suffering from depression. Such individuals are more likely to process, store, and retrieve event memories that resulted in negative feelings.

Q: What can be inferred from the passage?
(a) Our mood dictates which memories we recall.
(b) Most people have control over which events they remember.
(c) The theory of emotional memory predicts psychological disorders.
(d) Negatively charged memories are subdued by the subconscious mind.

36. In the last few decades, science papers advocating an evolutionary link between birds and dinosaurs have proliferated. More recently, however, the tide appears to be turning. Oregon State University, for instance, just published a study comparing the skeletal structure of birds and dinosaurs. It pinpoints an important difference between the two. The skeletal structure of birds requires a specific position of the thigh bone to allow the animals sufficient capacity for their lungs to expand. This characteristic is absent in the skeletons of most dinosaurs.

Q: What can be inferred from the passage?
(a) The Oregon State University study was flawed.
(b) Dinosaurs on average had larger lungs than birds do.
(c) The study suggests that birds did not evolve directly from dinosaurs.
(d) The position of the thigh bone is related to the size of the animal.

37. We citizens must start demanding more from our elected leaders. It's looking like the senator who recently admitted to having an extramarital affair is not going to resign. The senate chose to censure his actions but did not ask him to step down. I feel it is now up to us to see that this dishonest man is removed from office. Allowing him to remain in power sends a message to the rest of the world that we tolerate corruption in our government.

Q: What can be inferred from the passage?
(a) The writer first exposed the senator's affair.
(b) The senator will not choose to resign on his own.
(c) The writer once supported the senator in question.
(d) The senator has been convicted of misconduct before.

Part III Questions 38—40

Read the passage. Then identify the option that does NOT belong.

38. Everyone wants to live a longer life, but the truth is our social services are already buckling under the pressures of a growing elderly population. (a) Today, the average person lives around 75 years, but experts say this number is set to rise. (b) Health-care costs in the form of taxes climb as more government money is spent to care for the old. (c) But perhaps the most serious problem is the shortage of trained health-care personnel in comparison to the numbers of elderly. (d) These problems must be addressed quickly, or our entire health-care system faces the prospect of collapse.

39. MeetingWeb is a valuable tool for businesses in need of a platform to conduct virtual meetings. (a) With nothing more than computers and headsets, dispersed employees can interact as if they were in the same room together. (b) Audio and video synchronization enables real-time chatting, while MeetingWeb's robust server allows the sharing and transfer of large files. (c) Companies that act now may qualify for special discounts on this and other MeetingWeb products. (d) Best of all, with the Group Desktop function, all invited participants can access a communal desktop from their computers.

40. When the 6,880 concertgoers entered Hampton Memorial Auditorium last Friday evening, they had no idea they'd be witnessing the birth of a star. (a) The show was the first public performance by teenage hip-hop artist Alex Sharp. (b) From the opening number, Sharp had the entire building on its feet, grooving along to his infectious beats. (c) The highlight for many came during the encore, when he sang a medley of three popular R&B covers. (d) Sharp had performed previously at private functions, but had not encountered anything so untoward.

This is the end of the Reading Comprehension section. Please remain seated until the proctor has instructed otherwise. You are NOT allowed to turn to any other section of the test.

Actual Test 2

Listening Comprehension 💿CD

Grammar

Vocabulary

Reading Comprehension

LISTENING
COMPREHENSION

Part I **Questions 1—15**

You will now hear fifteen conversation fragments, each made up of a single spoken statement followed by four spoken responses. Choose the most appropriate response to the statement.

Part II **Questions 16—30**

You will now hear fifteen conversation fragments, each made up of three spoken statements followed by four spoken responses. Choose the most appropriate response to complete the conversation.

Part III **Questions 31—45**

You will now hear fifteen complete conversations. For each item, you will hear a conversation and its corresponding question, both of which will be read twice. Then you will hear four options which will be read only once. Choose the option that best answers the question.

Part IV **Questions 46—60**

You will now hear fifteen spoken monologues. For each item, you will hear a monologue and its corresponding question, both of which will be read twice. Then you will hear four options which will be read only once. Choose the option that best answers the question.

GRAMMAR

Part I **Questions 1—20**

Choose the best answer for the blank.

1. A: You know, _____.

B: The paintings were so powerful, weren't they?

(a) really that art exhibit I moved
(b) I really moved that art exhibit
(c) art exhibit that moved me really
(d) that art exhibit really moved me

2. A: Do you listen to much music?

B: Yes, I always have my earphones in while _____.

(a) I've exercised
(b) I'm exercising
(c) I'd exercised
(d) I'll be exercising

3. A: This math class is a pain, if you ask me.

B: I don't know. I kind of like _____ equations.

(a) solve
(b) solving
(c) to be solved
(d) the solution

4. A: What's the matter with Kate? She seems _____.

B: She lost her cell phone yesterday and has to buy a new one.

(a) agitated
(b) agitating
(c) to agitate
(d) to have agitated

5. A: Who wants to come with me to the film premier tonight?

B: _____! What time does it start?

(a) Do I
(b) I do
(c) I do it
(d) Do it

6. A: Have you seen the remote control lately?

B: I left it _____ the table the last time I used it.

(a) of
(b) on
(c) in
(d) to

7. A: Kelly's performance has been outstanding recently.

B: Yes. _____ a new contract, but her sales have been off the chart.

(a) Only closing she did not
(b) She only did not close
(c) Not only did she close
(d) She closed not only

8. A: Where _____? I've been calling for hours.

B: Sorry, I was stuck in traffic on the interstate.

(a) having been
(b) have you been
(c) you have been
(d) are you having

9. A: I can't believe you quit your job.
   B: Well, life's too short for me _____ my time with that company.

   (a) wasting
   (b) to be wasting
   (c) having wasted
   (d) I have wasted

10. A: Where's Arnold? It's not like him to be so late.
    B: He _____ we were meeting at your apartment.

    (a) can think
    (b) should think
    (c) should be thinking
    (d) must have thought

11. A: I can't believe I ate all the cookies. I just _____ help myself.
    B: Don't worry. They were actually low in fat and relatively healthy.

    (a) hadn't
    (b) wouldn't
    (c) couldn't
    (d) shouldn't

12. A: Have you decided which shoes to buy?
    B: Not quite, but I've narrowed it down to the _____ pairs.

    (a) sturdy two brown
    (b) two sturdy brown
    (c) two brown sturdy
    (d) brown sturdy two

13. A: What kind of format do you recommend for the essay, Professor?
    B: _____ you want to structure it is fine with me.

    (a) However
    (b) Whatever
    (c) Whichever
    (d) Wherever

14. A: Can you tell where the noise is coming from?
    B: Well, it sounds like it's originating somewhere in _____ rear of the vehicle.

    (a) a
    (b) the
    (c) that
    (d) this

15. A: Are you sure everyone is ready for the product launch?
    B: Yes, all of the department heads _____.

    (a) are alerting
    (b) have been alerted
    (c) are to have alerted
    (d) having been alerted

16. A: Today's the big day. Let me know _____.
    B: I'll call you as soon as I get out of class.

    (a) how the exam goes
    (b) how goes the exam
    (c) the exam how it goes
    (d) how the exam's going

17. A: This jacket's on sale, but it'll never fit me.

B: You might _____ try it on. You never know.

(a) as
(b) well
(c) well as
(d) as well

18. A: Can you tell me _____ enrollment for the course has opened yet?

B: I don't believe it has, but let me check.

(a) whether
(b) when
(c) like
(d) such

19. A: Tom is always late! I can't stand it!

B: _____, he's not very responsible.

(a) I've always said it's like
(b) It's like I've always said
(c) Like I've always said it is
(d) Always I've said like it

20. A: When is Darryl Adams going to release a new book?

B: _____? It takes time for talented writers to finish a novel.

(a) Who says
(b) Says who
(c) Can who say
(d) Who can say

Part II **Questions 21—40**

Choose the best answer for the blank.

21. Penicillin is a type of antibiotic that _____ in 1928 and led to cures for many serious diseases.

(a) discovered
(b) had discovered
(c) was discovered
(d) had been discovered

22. _____ a scholarship would mean nearly an 85% discount on yearly tuition.

(a) Securing
(b) Secured
(c) Securely
(d) Secure

23. With a mixture of mammalian and reptilian traits, the platypus is considered _____ Earth's most unique animals.

(a) of the
(b) the one
(c) one of
(d) only the

24. Addicts of the drug nicotine may exhibit _____ irritability, headaches, and nausea during the withdrawal period.

(a) symptoms as such
(b) as such symptoms
(c) symptoms such as
(d) as symptoms such

25. This lecture hall _____ one of the university's founders.

(a) names to get
(b) from a name got
(c) gets its name from
(d) is getting from a name

26. The judge ordered _____ payment for all outstanding traffic tickets under penalty of arrest.

(a) the man to remit
(b) that the man remitting
(c) for the man remit
(d) that the man remitted

27. Immigration authorities may not allow you into the country _____ proof of onward travel.

(a) without
(b) unless
(c) although
(d) barring

28. An updated university policy asserts that students shall _____ to retake exams only in the case of a medical emergency.

(a) permit
(b) be permitting
(c) be permitted
(d) have permitted

29. Taking aesthetically pleasing photographs is _____, regardless of how much experience they have.

(a) anything nobody can do
(b) nothing that everyone can do
(c) not something everyone can do
(d) everyone that can do anything

30. In the Crimean War of the 1850s, Britain allied with France so _____ prevent the Russians from gaining power in Turkey.

(a) to
(b) as
(c) to as
(d) as to

31. His clients are demanding that he _____ them with more accurate and timely invoices.

(a) provides
(b) provide
(c) provided
(d) is providing

32. The boundary between Europe and Asia is demarcated by the Ural Mountains, _____ run from north to south at roughly 60 degrees east.

(a) whose
(b) which
(c) where
(d) of which

33. Typos and other small errors plague even _____ text.

(a) the most closely edited
(b) a most closely editing
(c) most closely editing
(d) few most closely edited

34. More information about the project's creators _____ in the "about" section of their website.

(a) is found
(b) is finding
(c) were found
(d) has been finding

35. To protest women's lack of voting rights, Susan B. Anthony cast an illegal ballot in the 1872 presidential election and _____ subsequently arrested.

(a) to be
(b) was
(c) had been
(d) being

36. One of the most recognizable features of the film noir genre is the absence of _____ defined morals.

(a) clearly
(b) clearing
(c) clear
(d) clearer

37. The astronomical association's decision to overturn Pluto's status as a planet _____ thousands of science textbooks obsolete.

(a) is rendered
(b) got rendered
(c) rendered
(d) render

38. Despite studying for only a few hours, Rebecca reported that she found the test _____.

(a) more easily
(b) easy
(c) an easier
(d) easily

39. Though still undecided, Max is determined that he will major _____ in biology or biochemistry.

(a) either
(b) both
(c) neither
(d) nor

40. _____ for military research, we might never have realized that the ocean floor is not perfectly flat.

(a) It have been
(b) Being it had
(c) Hadn't it been
(d) Had it not been

Identify the option that contains an awkward expression or an error in grammar.

41. (a) A: How are you taking your final? Did you choose the essay or exam option?
    (b) B: To be honest, I still haven't made my decision.
    (c) A: Well, you have to tell the professor today, so you would better think fast.
    (d) B: I know. I'm simply not looking forward to either one.

42. (a) A: Did you pick up the invitations for the wedding yet?
    (b) B: No. I heard there was a delay with the printer and they're not ready yet.
    (c) A: I hope they do them soon. Time's running out!
    (d) B: Don't worry. Everything will sort out itself.

43. (a) A: More break time would mean increased productivity, in my opinion.
    (b) B: Too badly the boss doesn't agree with you.
    (c) A: I've printed out a report that should change his mind.
    (d) B: I'd give it a rest, if I were you.

44. (a) A: Michael's game starts at 3 tomorrow. Did you tell Liz to come?
    (b) B: I did, as she has another appointment.
    (c) A: That's too bad. This is his last match of the season.
    (d) B: Maybe we can videotape it for her.

45. (a) A: Was that the hotel on the phone?
    (b) B: Yes. They booked our room for the wrong date, and nothing else is available for tomorrow.
    (c) A: What? They gave us hard any warning at all!
    (d) B: It's not fair, but I guess we'll have to look for another hotel.

46. (a) Experts say eating habits we fall into as children often stick with us our entire lives. (b) Reflected objectively on the nutritional problems I experience today, I can't help but agree with that notion. (c) As a child, my parents didn't have the money to feed me right. (d) Fast food and junk food were centerpieces of my diet, just as they are today.

47. (a) Though practiced by many cultures, the rain dance is perhaps most strongly associated with Native North Americans. (b) Many of their communities still observe the ceremony each August, when the climate is driest. (c) In most cases, special clothing is worn, including spiritually significant masks and headdresses. (d) These outfits are made specifically for the occasion and storing safely away for the rest of the year.

48. (a) The town of Wittenoom in Western Australia has ceased but all to exist. (b) In the early 1960s it was home to around 20,000 people, but the government shut it down in 1966 due to contamination from the nearby asbestos mine. (c) Since then, nearly 2,000 people have died from conditions caused by exposure to asbestos. (d) Oddly, though, eight residents continue to live in Wittenoom, refusing to leave their homes no matter what the cost.

49. (a) Today, non-Hispanic whites make up the majority of the population of the United States, accounting for 66%. (b) However, in the year 2050, the country's demographic composition will look quite different. (c) By then, the Hispanic population will grow to represent 30% of the total. (d) Combined with the populations of African Americans and Asian Americans, they will transform the U.S. into a truly minority nation.

50. (a) When we make an error in speech that seems likely to have been influenced by a subconscious desire, it is called a "Freudian slip." (b) The phenomenon is named after the psychologist Sigmund Freud, who studied how our subconscious mind affects our conscious actions. (c) According to him, we possess desires that our conscious mind is unaware of. (d) Sometimes, these desires make them known through so-called "slips of the tongue."

VOCABULARY

Part I   Questions 1—25

Choose the best answer for the blank.

1. A: _____ a second, will you?
    I need to find my jacket.
    B: Isn't that on the back of your chair?

    (a) Hold on
    (b) Carry on
    (c) Go on
    (d) Take on

2. A: My throat's pretty sore, but I'm sure it'll be better tomorrow.
    B: No, you should see the doctor. It's best not to take any _____.

    (a) possibilities
    (b) opportunities
    (c) chances
    (d) accidents

3. A: Brian is still upset at me for losing his CD.
    B: It's been three months. He should really _____ it.

    (a) pass through
    (b) settle on
    (c) get over
    (d) cut out

4. A: You can't sit back and wait for your computer to _____ fix itself.
    B: I'm not. I just got off the phone with tech support.

    (a) impressively
    (b) miraculously
    (c) formally
    (d) grudgingly

5. A: Wow, you really _____.
    B: I know. I can't believe the professor didn't catch my error!

    (a) caught up
    (b) paid off
    (c) lucked out
    (d) dove in

6. A: How do I deposit this paycheck?
    B: First you have to _____ the back.

    (a) advance
    (b) endorse
    (c) promote
    (d) improve

7. A: The bank's _____ of the home put its value at $320,000.
    B: Oh no, that's much too low.

    (a) appraisal
    (b) renewal
    (c) loan
    (d) preview

8. A: Can I try a slice of the pie?
    B: Sure. Let me know how it _____.

    (a) savors
    (b) tastes
    (c) flavors
    (d) bakes

9. A: Are you going to live on campus next semester?

    B: No, I'm going _____ for the whole year.

    (a) abroad
    (b) worldly
    (c) outside
    (d) afar

10. A: I'm sorry. I just don't care for the picture.

    B: That's okay. Thanks for speaking your _____.

    (a) mind
    (b) idea
    (c) thought
    (d) negative

11. A: We had to take my father to the hospital last night. It's his heart.

    B: My _____. Is there anything I can do?

    (a) reminiscences
    (b) condolences
    (c) acquaintances
    (d) incidences

12. A: Let's take a taxi downtown instead of riding the subway.

    B: I can't. I don't have enough money for cab _____.

    (a) fare
    (b) price
    (c) fee
    (d) charge

13. A: I _____ you don't mind my joining you tonight.

    B: Of course not. The more, the merrier!

    (a) know
    (b) find
    (c) agree
    (d) hope

14. A: What time do you want to meet tomorrow?

    B: Whenever is most _____ for you. I'm flexible.

    (a) optimistic
    (b) elastic
    (c) sufficient
    (d) convenient

15. A: You can see the stars so clearly out here in the country.

    B: I know. Look at how they _____.

    (a) revolve
    (b) sparkle
    (c) oscillate
    (d) wiggle

16. A: The quality of this writing is simply _____.

    B: I'll speak to Richard about putting more effort into his work.

    (a) unaffordable
    (b) unavailable
    (c) unacceptable
    (d) unachievable

17. A: What did you think of the remake of the film?

B: I liked the _____ much better.

(a) original
(b) standard
(c) precedent
(d) creation

18. A: This bus is _____ for Detroit, isn't it?

B: Yes, by way of Chicago.

(a) filled
(b) bound
(c) made
(d) settled

19. A: Can you believe this drought?

B: I know. Today is the city's 43rd _____ day in a row.

(a) hot
(b) dry
(c) mild
(d) bright

20. A: What happened to your paragraph on ancient glassmaking?

B: The essay was running long, so I _____.

(a) mixed it up
(b) set it down
(c) left it out
(d) moved it over

21. A: Does the room have a safe?

B: Yes. You're advised to store your _____ belongings there.

(a) costly
(b) valuable
(c) scarce
(d) worthwhile

22. A: Did you _____ a check with the tax form?

B: Yes, I did. Everything's there in the envelope.

(a) enclose
(b) adhere
(c) salute
(d) contain

23. A: I don't approve of the layoffs, but we have no other choice.

B: Looks like we'll have to _____ the bullet.

(a) chew
(b) bite
(c) eat
(d) slurp

24. A: Don't you think 30 years in jail is a little harsh?

B: Well, he did _____ investors out of millions.

(a) swindle
(b) mystify
(c) gesture
(d) boggle

25. A: I can't seem to decide which of these jobs to accept.

B: Follow your _____ instinct, as I always say.

(a) feet
(b) body
(c) stomach
(d) gut

Part II **Questions 26—50**

Choose the best answer for the blank.

26. The Association of Practicing Physicians is concerned by the rise in the infant mortality _____.

(a) tempo
(b) rate
(c) proportion
(d) degree

27. One of the more _____ elements of Gothic architecture is the use of stained glass depicting scenes from the Bible.

(a) ornamental
(b) husky
(c) rugged
(d) subsistent

28. The Free Laptop Foundation aims to address the _____ in computer access between rich and poor.

(a) disparity
(b) penchant
(c) illustration
(d) amenity

29. Customers _____ after-sales service as the area in which we need the most improvement.

(a) summoned
(b) quoted
(c) extracted
(d) cited

30. There is little point in initiating a diet if you have no intention of _____ to it.

(a) following
(b) staying
(c) sticking
(d) coming

31. Lower _____ payments for first-time homebuyers is perhaps the only positive result of the current downturn.

(a) rent
(b) maintenance
(c) interest
(d) vaudeville

32. In addition to being an award-winning author, Ernest Hemingway was a(n) _____ traveler, frequenting Europe, the Caribbean, and Africa.

(a) tepid
(b) staple
(c) avid
(d) insidious

33. _____ the cleansing power of Brite Tile with other leading brands and we're sure you'll agree: Brite's the best.

(a) Separate
(b) Compare
(c) Obscure
(d) Mediate

34. China's first manned spaceflight in 2003 made it the third country in the world to have succeeded in such a(n) _____.

    (a) venture
    (b) speculation
    (c) occupation
    (d) lineup

35. The practical _____ of sociological research are numerous, from overhauling education systems to solving crime.

    (a) applications
    (b) connotations
    (c) exonerations
    (d) manipulations

36. High tannin content gives red wines a bitter and often _____ taste to the uninitiated drinker.

    (a) excruciating
    (b) drastic
    (c) unsavory
    (d) tempestuous

37. In dispersed communities located far from power transmission lines, solar technology _____ a viable alternative for the supply of electricity.

    (a) assumes
    (b) expresses
    (c) corresponds
    (d) represents

38. According to the terms of the lawsuit, the funds will be _____ to the victim at monthly intervals by the accountant.

    (a) dispersed
    (b) concentrated
    (c) revoked
    (d) solicited

39. Following a string of military defeats in the sixteenth century, much of Serbia was _____ into the Ottoman Empire.

    (a) pursued
    (b) absorbed
    (c) enacted
    (d) contributed

40. Having overheard news of the hostile takeover, the CEO came to the negotiating table with an ax to _____.

    (a) wield
    (b) grind
    (c) sharpen
    (d) chop

41. In a questionable move, the presidential candidate selected an obscure state senator to be his running _____.

    (a) mate
    (b) primate
    (c) double
    (d) confusion

42. Flashes of lightning that occur on the distant horizon and are unaccompanied by the sound of thunder are often _____ to as "heat lightning."

    (a) credited
    (b) referred
    (c) paraded
    (d) replied

43. Lucille Ball, star of the sitcom *I Love Lucy*, remains one of the most _____ symbols of U.S. popular culture.

    (a) enduring
    (b) responsible
    (c) heightened
    (d) comfortable

44. Some hand gestures regarded as _____ in one's home country may be found deeply offensive in others.

    (a) mordant
    (b) voracious
    (c) distinctive
    (d) innocuous

45. After _____ the corporation loyally for over 20 years, Mr. Reynolds was awarded a generous early retirement package.

    (a) lathering
    (b) gripping
    (c) passing
    (d) serving

46. To better _____ the status of its shipments, the company has outfitted its trucks with GPS receivers.

    (a) stalk
    (b) expose
    (c) track
    (d) capture

47. The government continually _____ it is doing all it can to weed out corruption.

    (a) requests
    (b) insists
    (c) demands
    (d) urges

48. For turkeys under ten pounds, common wisdom _____ that they should be roasted for twenty minutes per pound.

    (a) holds
    (b) believes
    (c) regards
    (d) feels

49. Self-reflection, tranquility, and inner peace are all qualities associated with the practice of _____.

    (a) celebration
    (b) insulation
    (c) origination
    (d) meditation

50. Desert plant and animal species have evolved various biological _____ that enable them to survive in an otherwise inhospitable environment.

    (a) principles
    (b) mechanisms
    (c) devices
    (d) proxies

This is the end of the Vocabulary section. Do NOT move on to the Reading Comprehension section until instructed to do so. You are NOT allowed to turn to any other section of the test.

READING
COMPREHENSION

Part I **Questions 1—16**

Read the passage. Then choose the option that best completes the passage.

---

1. In literature, magic realism weaves fantastical elements into stories of everyday life. Characters within this genre inhabit realistic settings yet do not regard the magical occurrences as out of the ordinary. Magic realism is seen most often in Latin American literature, where cultural folktales provide the inspiration for supernatural beings and events. The genre allows authors to question social conventions or government policies without incurring the censorship such critiques would face were they

      _____.

      (a) leveled in a more direct fashion
      (b) aimed instead at a culture's myths
      (c) offered through a different medium
      (d) endorsed by artists in various fields

2. The name Alexander Graham Bell is widely recognized as belonging to the inventor of the telephone. Yet, Bell's famous creation was an unintended consequence of his experimentation with one of his true passions: helping the deaf and mute. Both his mother and wife had lost their hearing and played a large role in motivating Bell's work. It was through his efforts to develop a rudimentary hearing aid for the deaf that he came up with the concept of the telephone. Later in life, Bell avoided keeping a phone in his workshop, regarding it as a _____.

      (a) youthful error in judgment
      (b) useless piece of technology
      (c) distraction from his true calling
      (d) financial failure and a disappointment

3. It can be difficult for an individual to understand _____.
      Many health advocates recommend that the average person drink at minimum two liters of water every 24 hours to avoid dehydration. Other medical professionals, however, put the figure much lower, at just one liter per day. Moreover, an individual's need for water can vary greatly according to body type and size, weather conditions, and the nature and duration of physical activities undertaken.

      (a) the serious health risks of dehydration
      (b) how much water he or she should consume
      (c) how his or her body uses the water that is drunk
      (d) the latest research findings on water consumption

4.

> Dear valuable customer,
>
> The editorial staff at *Design Monthly* would like to make you aware of an exciting new offer. For a limited time only, a month-long subscription to our award-winning architectural magazine is available for just $26.99. That's a savings of over $30 off the newsstand price! _____, simply fill out the enclosed order form and mail it in to us. You won't regret it!
>
> Gratefully yours,
> *Design Monthly* editorial staff

(a) To help with this incredible survey
(b) If you have an interest in modern landscaping
(c) To be removed from the *Design Monthly* mailing list
(d) If you choose to take advantage of this one-time deal

5. The Mongol Empire was the largest continuous empire the world has ever known, spanning nearly a quarter of Earth's land area. It was initiated by the legendary Genghis Khan and spread quickly from its heart in modern-day Mongolia. Extending from the East Sea to Europe's Danube River, and from the Arctic to tropical Southeast Asia, it ruled over 100 million people in its heyday. However, the empire's great size ultimately led to its undoing. Succession struggles after Genghis' death led to civil wars, _____.

(a) and the once mighty empire split apart
(b) but the empire's dominance lasted for centuries
(c) as each Mongol general expanded the empire
(d) for a united Mongolia was important to the Mongols

6. I have nothing against portable music players. In fact, I own one of the latest models and enjoy listening to it during my morning subway commute. What I don't approve of is the use of these players by bicyclists. Part of being a responsible bicycle rider is being aware of your surroundings, but how can you if you can't hear the horn of the car you just cut off? Cyclists have gotten the message about helmet safety. Now it's time to tell them to _____!

(a) take off those earphones
(b) travel with more awareness
(c) keep their bikes maintained
(d) commute by subway instead

7. In terms of cargo tonnage, which is the measure of the weight of all goods loaded and unloaded, _____. Located as it is in proximity to one of China's most developed and economically vital cities, Shanghai's port is the primary point of exit and entry for products involved in China's vast trade networks. Prior to 2005, the ports of Singapore and Rotterdam offered competition for the cargo tonnage title. But, reflecting the continued growth of China's economic might, Shanghai has since overtaken both of them.

    (a) several ports are overtaking Shanghai
    (b) the port of Shanghai is the world's busiest
    (c) Shanghai is a relatively newly established port
    (d) Shanghai imports less cargo than it used to

8. In the early 1980s, video games consisted of a large, upright box with a video monitor, joystick, and a few buttons—what was known as an arcade game. The logistics of play were quite limited, as were the games themselves. Today, consoles no larger than a textbook utilize motion sensors to remotely transmit a player's movements and commands to the game. Where controllers are used, they are complex and comprehensive, and the selection of games is seemingly infinite. Clearly,

    _____.

    (a) video games have undergone a drastic transformation
    (b) these games are much more popular than they once were
    (c) video game production has become a profitable industry
    (d) advances in technology have made arcade games obsolete

9. Tired of traipsing around town with your laptop, trying to find a wireless network to get online? Then Catalyst Electronics has some good news for you, as they're introducing the iWi, the world's first portable personal network device. Simply insert the iWi card into your laptop and a wi-fi "bubble" will instantly form around you, allowing you to connect securely and reliably to the Internet. Never again will you have to _____.

    (a) leave home with your laptop
    (b) reboot to take advantage of wi-fi
    (c) hunt for that elusive network signal
    (d) worry about compromising your privacy

10. Lasik—or laser-eye surgery, as it is commonly known—is a type of refractive surgery that utilizes a laser beam. As in all refractive surgeries, the goal is to modify the dimensions of the patient's cornea in order to correct naturally developing vision problems. In a Lasik procedure, these modifications are made with a precisely directed and controlled Excimer laser. Though some remain skeptical, concerned about long-term damage, _____.

(a) the technology behind Lasik surgeries is brand new
(b) human eyes have proven resistant to the damage caused
(c) the procedure has yet to be approved by medical associations
(d) thousands of Lasik operations have been performed successfully

11. When considering adolescent males, _____. Those who reach puberty first will typically grow taller and stronger in the coming years than their late-blooming peers. For this reason, they tend to develop a better body image and are more comfortable with their appearance. On the other hand, the early onset of puberty can make boys aggressive and unpredictable due to increased hormone levels. In addition, because they look more like adults, these adolescents will often be assumed to possess more developed emotional states to match their physical progress. This, of course, is usually not the case.

(a) the onset of puberty brings many difficulties
(b) the timing of puberty determines their personalities
(c) there are positives and negatives to early maturation
(d) much about their maturation process remains a mystery

12. The name "comic book" was coined because the earliest manifestations were nothing more than collections of humorous newspaper-style comic strips. The term is still in use today, despite the fact that _____. In America, the super-hero genre is most popular, with titles such as *Superman*, *Spiderman*, and *X-Men*. Japanese and European comic books feature real-life situations, and their content tends to be more dramatic.

(a) most modern comics are serious in tone
(b) the market for comics has since expanded
(c) the popularity of comics is at an all-time low
(d) fewer people read newspapers than in the past

13. For a period of roughly 100 years beginning in the 1860s, millions of Italians emigrated from their homeland. The driving force behind this mass migration was poverty, as conditions for poor farmers living in the Italian countryside were harsh. The majority of emigrants headed for either North or South America, but many others chose destinations within Europe and also Australia. Regardless of where they went, they always brought their traditions with them. The result is that many locales, from New York to Brazil to New Zealand, _____.

(a) no longer allow immigration by Italians
(b) encouraged their citizens to settle in Italy
(c) became prosperous thanks to Italian laborers
(d) have been heavily influenced by Italian culture

14. When a patient is suffering from a bacterial infection, common practice is to administer an antibiotic to neutralize the bacteria. What medical professionals are beginning to discover, however, is that over time strains of bacteria can evolve a resistance to overused antibiotics. These so-called "superbugs" present a dangerous new challenge to medicine. What once may have been considered a relatively harmless infection could become a life-threatening condition. For now, the focus is on preventing the evolution of superbugs in the first place, _____.

(a) something doctors have long advocated
(b) meaning more judicious use of antibiotics
(c) through the use of a new class of medicine
(d) and keeping patients on antibiotic treatments

15. Among increasing consensus that large-scale, top-down models of foreign aid have failed to produce results and may even be causing more harm than good, a new approach is gaining acceptance. Microfinance projects are popping up in all corners of the developing world, and some hope they will one day replace government-gifted aid altogether. Proponents point out that supporting local small businesses via microloans is the best way to promote financial responsibility and economic growth in the third world. _____, people take better care of things they've earned themselves than things simply given them.

   (a) Yet
   (b) After all
   (c) Nonetheless
   (d) In spite of that

16. In the late summer and fall of 2006, several Southeast Asian nations experienced one of the worst air pollution events in their histories. Unfettered slash-and-burn agricultural operations in rural Indonesia created a haze that overwhelmed skies over Malaysia, Thailand, and as far north as South Korea. In addition to affecting visibility, the haze contained a number of toxic compounds, such as sulfuric acid. Regional governments accused Indonesia's leaders of complicity in the burning. _____, the truth is that the country's officials had little power to control the actions of corporate farmers and private landowners.

   (a) However
   (b) Likewise
   (c) Moreover
   (d) Therefore

Read the passage and the question. Then choose the option that best answers the question.

17. Computer files are bigger than ever these days, and transferring them from computer to computer can present a real dilemma if the machines are not connected via a network. Standard email accounts impose strict file size limits, and even physical storage media such as CDs may be inadequate. To address this need, several companies offer online transfer services. All a user needs to do is upload the file to the company's server, and then the website delivers a download invitation to the recipient. In the beginning, companies charged for this service, but now there are many free alternatives.

Q: What is the best title for the passage?

(a) The Limitations of Email
(b) A New Way to Swap Files
(c) Sharing Files via a Network
(d) Zero-Cost Software Options

18. Dog owners know there are times when their dogs are far from man's best friend. So, to help your dog live up to his or her potential, obedience training is essential. At Northpark Canine Academy, we do more than just teach your dog to sit, stay, and roll over. Our methods have been certified by the American Kennel Club to produce animals that will comply with your every command. We'll make sure your dog remains your best friend.

Q: What is mainly being advertised?

(a) A learning program for dog owners
(b) A training institution for dogs
(c) A certified method of pet training
(d) A dog-care service for busy owners

19. Many English students are familiar with Shakespeare's plays, with works such as *Hamlet* and *Romeo and Juliet* featured on many curricula. But fewer may be aware that the famous bard also penned over 150 sonnets. The poems, originally published in a single collection in 1609, deal primarily with the subjects of love and romance, and each of them adheres to the strict formatting standards that define the genre.

Q: What is the passage about?
(a) Poetry in Shakespeare's plays
(b) The style and format of sonnets
(c) Some lesser-known poetry of Shakespeare
(d) Shakespeare's preference of poetry over drama

20. Winter is fast approaching, and there's no time like the present to make sure your snow gear needs are satisfied. But why pay hundreds of dollars for new products in the store when you can get last year's models for up to 70% off from your friends and neighbors? That's why the East Rutherford Winter Gear Swap comes in. This Saturday, September 29, come to the City Auditorium to buy, sell, and trade used gear with your fellow East Rutherford citizens. You'll never know what kinds of deals await until you get here.

Q: What is being announced?
(a) A secondhand product exchange
(b) A yearly winter product exhibition
(c) A new gear outlet in East Rutherford
(d) A discount on name-brand winter gear

21. The two European members of World War II's Axis powers, Germany and Italy, had yet to warm to each other in the early 1930s. Mussolini, the leader of Italy, initially did not approve of the anti-Jewish and overall racist policies being forwarded by Germany's Adolf Hitler. As war approached, he even considered siding with the French against Germany. However, as Hitler consolidated his power, it became impossible for Mussolini to resist an alliance with the Nazis.

Q: What is the main idea of the passage?
(a) World War II created many unlikely alliances.
(b) Mussolini advised Hitler on his policies of race.
(c) Italy fought briefly against Germany during WWII.
(d) The Axis powers' pre-war relationship was tenuous.

22. If there were a "mother" of chemotherapy, it would be Polish physicist Marie Curie. Her studies in radioactivity—a term she created—led her to experiment for the first time with using radioactive isotopes to halt the growth of cancerous tumors. Her investigations into this powerful new medical tool, along with the radioactive chemical elements she discovered, profoundly affected scientists' understanding of our world. Sadly, Curie died at the age of 66 from exposure to radiation, but her legacy lives on in the millions of cancer patients who have been cured through chemotherapy.

Q: What is the best title for the passage?

(a) Curie and Chemotherapy: Her Tragic Story
(b) The Health Risks of Studying Radioactivity
(c) The Woman behind Modern Cancer Treatment
(d) Marie Curie and the Discovery of Radioactivity

23. One element that often goes unconsidered in the current debate on whaling is the cultural rights of indigenous peoples. For instance, the Makah people of America's Pacific Northwest have a long tradition of whaling for nutritional, communal, and spiritual purposes. Beginning in the 1920s, the Makah were prohibited from whale killing, a response to declining populations worldwide. However, in 1999, the U.S. government reinstituted the Makah's right to carry out their cultural tradition, granting permission for the hunting of one whale per year.

Q: Which of the following is correct about the Makah?

(a) The whales they hunted were usually eaten.
(b) They continued whaling in the '20s despite the ban.
(c) Their culture condones the hunting of most wild animals.
(d) The government prevents them from practicing their religion.

24. London's British Museum houses artifacts from all over the world, collected primarily during the zenith of the British Empire. Now, the countries from which these priceless historical items were taken are demanding that they be returned. Egypt, for example, would very much like to be able to display the famous Rosetta Stone in one of its domestic collections. The British Museum has refused the majority of such requests, arguing that its possession of foreign artifacts is protected under British law.

Q: Which of the following is correct according to the passage?

(a) Most British Museum artifacts are of British origin.
(b) The Rosetta Stone was removed from Egypt by the British.
(c) The Rosetta Stone is the British Museum's most prized item.
(d) The British Museum is willing to entertain the countries' claims.

25. World health monitoring bodies have long recommended the breastfeeding of infants as the best way to ensure their physical health. What there is less consensus on, however, is whether or not the practice has anything to do with a child's cognitive development. A series of studies carried out since 2000 offer up inconclusive results. Some have found that children who were breastfed for at least six months score up to seven points higher on intelligence tests, whereas others claim that no correlation exists between the two variables.

Q: Which of the following is correct about breastfeeding?
(a) It is the method that most infants prefer.
(b) It has no impact on a child's intelligence.
(c) It is sanctioned by most health authorities.
(d) It affects an infant's cognitive development.

26. When it comes to wind power, one country is clearly leading the way: Denmark. As an early adopter of wind turbine technology in the 1970s, Denmark quickly developed into not only the number-one producer of wind-generated electricity, but also the world's top manufacturer of wind turbines. Today, the Scandinavian nation meets just under 20% of its electricity needs via wind farms located both on land and at sea. Moreover, Danish firms like Vestas Wind Systems are responsible for almost half of global turbine manufacturing.

Q: Which of the following is correct according to the passage?
(a) No other nation has stronger winds than Denmark.
(b) Denmark was one of the first countries to embrace wind power.
(c) A majority of Danish manufacturers produce wind systems.
(d) Denmark plans to increase its wind-generated electricity output by 20%.

27. Musician and songwriter Nina Simone produced songs that were difficult to categorize. Though arguably classifiable under the general label of "jazz," Simone's many hits also mix elements of blues, gospel, soul, and even folk music. Her eclectic style was combined with a haunting and unusually low female singing voice, resulting in music that was truly memorable. Indeed, numerous modern artists cite Simone as one of their major inspirations.

Q: Which of the following is correct about Nina Simone?

(a) She had difficulty singing high notes.
(b) She did not meet with critical acclaim.
(c) She preferred jazz music to other genres.
(d) She influenced a number of later musicians.

28.

Dear Mr. Chairman,

I have been a member of the Rawlson Anthropological Society for six years and have thoroughly enjoyed receiving the society's newsletters and participating in discussions on anthropological issues. Unfortunately, a recent change in my financial situation will make it impossible for me to pay my annual membership dues of $75. For this reason, I must ask to be removed from the society roster for the coming year. Hopefully I will be in a position to rejoin next year.

Yours,
Melissa Block

Q: Which of the following is correct according to the letter?

(a) The society was founded six years ago.
(b) Ms. Block is a colleague of the society's chairman.
(c) The society collects a yearly fee from its members.
(d) Ms. Block hopes to continue receiving the newsletter.

29. The Tainos inhabited a number of Caribbean islands at the time of the arrival of Christopher Columbus and the Spanish conquest. Among the many cultural traits noted by the Spaniards was a sport played in all Taino communities called batey. Not unlike volleyball, it featured two opposing teams and a small rubber ball that was passed back and forth. The players, however, were not allowed to touch the ball with their hands. Instead, the shoulder, elbow, knee, head, and other body parts were used. More than simple recreation, batey matches seemed to function as a means of conflict resolution between neighboring villages.

Q: Which of the following is correct according to the passage?
(a) The Taino were a fit and athletic people.
(b) The Spanish participated in matches of batey.
(c) Batey was similar to a mix of volleyball and soccer.
(d) Batey opponents were always from different villages.

30. Though many airlines around the world are rushing to enable passengers to make in-flight cellular calls, the concept has encountered some unexpected turbulence in the U.S. For one thing, American service providers haven't yet resolved how to bill customers for making calls 30,000 feet in the air. But additionally, poll after poll shows that the majority of passengers frown on the idea. Just as cell use is discouraged in movie theaters and some restaurants, the image of one's seat neighbor blabbing away throughout the flight is not a pleasant prospect.

Q: Which of the following is correct according to the passage?
(a) The debate over cell use on airplanes has been settled.
(b) Americans would find inflight phone calls disruptive.
(c) U.S. air carriers do not approve of in-flight cell service.
(d) Making in-flight calls could be prohibitively expensive.

31. We think of HIV as a modern disease, but scientists believe similar illnesses have been plaguing mammals for the last 100 million years. Researchers have discovered traces of retroviruses—the class of virus to which HIV belongs—in the genetic coding of the two-toed sloth, a direct descendant of the oldest mammals. In fact, this puts the earliest known incidence of retroviruses at 100 million years ago, whereas before this finding scientists had dated them to just 15 million years old. It is hoped that studying the relationship between retroviruses and mammalian evolution will lead to more advanced treatments for HIV, or even a cure.

Q: Which of the following is correct about retroviruses?
(a) They first appeared 15 million years ago.
(b) They are a leading cause of death in sloths.
(c) They all result in fatal conditions in humans.
(d) They have evolved in parallel with mammals.

32. A major figure in the story of Antarctic exploration was Sir Ernest Shackleton. Shackleton's first journey to the southernmost continent came in 1901, and he returned six years later in an attempt to reach the South Pole. He failed, but his team came to within 100 miles of their target, the closest ever at that time. In 1914, he went back a third time with plans to traverse the continent from shore to shore. Despite his vessel being destroyed by sea ice, Shackleton and his entire crew survived for three years before being rescued.

Q: Which of the following is correct according to the passage?
(a) Antarctica had never been explored prior to 1901.
(b) Shackleton was the first to set foot on the South Pole.
(c) Shackleton overcame disaster during his 1914 voyage.
(d) The location of the South Pole was unknown to Shackleton.

33. Over the last 20 months, businesses nationwide have been going crazy over the Collins & Whitmore Problem Solving Program. More than 160,000 copies of the course materials have been sold, and it is estimated that as many as 1.6 million employees have been obliged by their companies to complete the program. Now that results are finally coming in, the truth is coming out. The average employee is no better at solving everyday workplace problems today than he or she was 20 months ago. Unfortunately for employers, Collins & Whitmore does not offer refunds.

Q: What can be inferred from the passage?
(a) The product in question has been used improperly.
(b) Collins & Whitmore's popularity continues to grow.
(c) Companies feel cheated by the problem solving course.
(d) A lack of problem solving skills plagues most businesses.

34. Anyone doubting the richness of Earth's biodiversity has only to travel to the jungles of Southeast Asia, where 63 new animal species were discovered in 2008 alone. The previously unknown creatures included a frog with fangs that preys on birds and a gecko with orange eyes and body stripes resembling a leopard. A new species of pit viper and a bird that seems disdainful of flying were also among the discoveries.

Q: What can be inferred from the passage?
(a) Most newly discovered species are reptiles.
(b) Southeast Asian countries are rich with wildlife.
(c) Most of the world's frogs live in Southeast Asia.
(d) An increase in studies by Asian biologists occurred in 2008.

35. In my opinion, the biggest problem with healthcare today is that there aren't enough skilled general practitioners. Doctors know they can make more money by becoming specialists in fields like cosmetic surgery or neurosurgery, so most end up there. To fix this problem, we need to address how doctors get paid. Physicians in general practice, who handle the highest percentage of patients, need to be making more than specialists, who don't help as large a percentage of the population.

Q: What can be inferred from the passage?

(a) Most general practitioners are not highly skilled.
(b) The author is a physician with a general practice.
(c) Physician pay scales have changed in recent years.
(d) The author believes general practitioners are treated unfairly.

36. "Buffalo Bill" Cody was a charismatic figure of the American West. He earned his nickname by killing 4,860 buffalo for eight months to feed the workers of the Kansas Pacific Railroad. Modern Cody fans highlight his support of Native American rights and the fact that he employed many Indians in the "Wild West" shows he produced. His detractors, on the other hand, label such shows as derogatory and finger Cody as a major player in the destruction of Native American culture.

Q: What can be inferred about "Buffalo Bill" Cody?

(a) His legacy is open to debate.
(b) His biggest fans were Indians.
(c) He was part Native American.
(d) He is usually remembered fondly.

37. To describe the process of socialization, sociologists often refer to two different stages: primary and secondary. Primary socialization involves children learning about the morals and norms of their society at large. For example, general guidelines for what behaviors a culture deems polite are picked up during primary socialization. Secondary socialization is more specific, dealing with the beliefs and behaviors of smaller groups—such as one's peers or coworkers—to which teenagers and adults belong.

Q: What can be inferred from the passage?

(a) Primary socialization occurs at a young age.
(b) Primary socialization is more difficult to study.
(c) Secondary socialization is not undergone by all.
(d) Secondary socialization teaches cultural taboos.

Part III **Questions 38—40**

Read the passage. Then identify the option that does NOT belong.

38. Americans searching for a bicycling adventure need to look no further than their own backyards. (a) The U.S. is home to a wide array of bike trails, no matter which region you live in. (b) Whether you want to cycle the entire Atlantic coast or just go for an off-road day ride, you're sure to find what you're looking for. (c) American-made bicycles have earned an impressive reputation for reliability and quality. (d) Check out the website of the American Cycling Association for specific route information.

39. The only woman ever to lead a Chinese dynasty was Empress Wu Zetian. (a) In the latter half of the 7th century A.D., she controlled the Chinese state through her husband, a Tang Dynasty emperor, and later her sons. (b) In 690 she seized the throne for herself, halting the Tang and initiating a new dynasty called the Zhou. (c) Despite their disapproval of her methods, later historians would admit that she was a capable ruler. (d) Shortly before her death in 705, she was overthrown and the Tang Dynasty was reestablished.

40. Contrary to popular opinion, the growth rate of humankind's global population is currently declining. (a) There were still less than one billion people alive on the planet in the year 1800. (b) A peak was reached in 1962 with 2.2% growth, and today that figure is over a full percentage point lower. (c) It is true that growth trends in many developing nations remain high. (d) On the other hand, the majority of Western industrialized nations are experiencing negative growth.

This is the end of the Reading Comprehension section. Please remain seated until the proctor has instructed otherwise. You are NOT allowed to turn to any other section of the test.

Actual Test 3

Listening Comprehension

Grammar

Vocabulary

Reading Comprehension

TEPS

LISTENING COMPREHENSION

DIRECTIONS

1. In the Listening Comprehension section, all content will be presented orally rather than in written form.

2. This section contains 4 parts. In parts I and II, each passage will be read only once. In parts III and IV, each passage and its corresponding question will be read twice. But in all sections, the options will be read only once. After listening to the passage and question, listen to the options and choose the best answer.

Part I   Questions 1—15

You will now hear fifteen conversation fragments, each made up of a single spoken statement followed by four spoken responses. Choose the most appropriate response to the statement.

Part II   Questions 16—30

You will now hear fifteen conversation fragments, each made up of three spoken statements followed by four spoken responses. Choose the most appropriate response to complete the conversation.

Part III **Questions 31—45**

You will now hear fifteen complete conversations. For each item, you will hear a conversation and its corresponding question, both of which will be read twice. Then you will hear four options which will be read only once. Choose the option that best answers the question.

Part IV **Questions 46—60**

You will now hear fifteen spoken monologues. For each item, you will hear a monologue and its corresponding question, both of which will be read twice. Then you will hear four options which will be read only once. Choose the option that best answers the question.

GRAMMAR

DIRECTIONS

This part of the exam tests your grammar skills. You will have 25 minutes to complete the 50 questions. Be sure to follow the directions given by the proctor.

Part I Questions 1—20

Choose the best answer for the blank.

1. A: Why do you go to the gym every day, Jules?

    B: I enjoy _____.

    (a) exercising
    (b) to exercise
    (c) being exercised
    (d) having been exercised

2. A: _____ Jack calls tonight, I'll ask him to come over.

    B: Great! I'm looking forward to seeing him again.

    (a) As
    (b) So
    (b) Until
    (d) When

3. A: Did anyone cheat in your final exam yesterday?

    B: No chance. The proctor _____ at the front of the room.

    (a) had everyone leave their bag
    (b) got everyone leave their bags
    (c) got everyone leaving their bag
    (d) had to everyone leave bags

4. A: Justin, how was the marathon?

    B: Pretty good. I finished in under four hours and _____.

    (a) so Bryan did
    (b) so did Bryan
    (c) also did Bryan
    (d) also Bryan did

5. A: Did your brother go to the rally this evening?

    B: Yes, and now _____.

    (a) he is arrested
    (b) he has been arrested
    (c) he had been arrested
    (d) he should have been arrested

6. A: Do you think Jin Soo has been invited to the wedding?

    B: I don't know, but _____.

    (a) I hope it
    (b) I hope so
    (c) I will hope it
    (d) I would be hoping

7. A: What are you looking for?

    B: I can't find my diamond earrings. I think _____.

    (a) they steal
    (b) they've stolen
    (c) they were stealing
    (d) they've been stolen

8. A: Do you like strong black coffee?

    B: Not usually, but I liked _____ we had this morning.

    (a) coffee
    (b) a coffee
    (c) the coffee
    (d) some coffee

9. A: The burglar put a hole in the wall.

B: _____ to get into the safe.

(a) Definitely he was trying
(b) He was definitely trying
(c) Trying he was definitely
(d) He was trying definitely

10. A: What was your physics final like?

B: It was horrible. In fact, it _____ worse.

(a) can't be
(b) couldn't be
(c) can't have been
(d) couldn't have been

11. A: It looks really dirty in here. How often are these offices _____?

B: Twice a week, sir.

(a) cleaned
(b) cleaning
(c) to clean
(d) been cleaned

12. A: Do you agree that money can't buy happiness?

B: No. _____.

(a) Richer I get, happier I am
(b) Richer I get, more I am happy
(c) The richer I get, the happier I am
(d) The more rich I get, the more happy I am

13. A: What was your wedding dress like?

B: It was a _____ gown.

(a) short off-white beautiful satin
(b) beautiful satin short off-white
(c) short satin off-white beautiful
(d) beautiful short off-white satin

14. A: How was your flight to Australia?

B: Terrible. The traffic was so heavy that _____ the bus, but we missed our plane as well.

(a) we not only missing
(b) not only we did miss
(c) not only did we miss
(d) we had not only missed

15. A: I've heard your brother is studying piano at college. _____?

B: He's better than me, but not outstanding.

(a) How good pianist is he
(b) How good is he pianist
(c) How is he a good pianist
(d) How good a pianist is he

16. A: _____ your new job!

B: Thank you very much.

(a) Congratulations on
(b) Congratulation on
(c) Congratulations for
(d) Congratulation for

17. A: Your new Italian boyfriend cooked dinner for you?

B: Yes. He asked his mother _____.

  (a) how pizza to make
  (b) how to make pizza
  (c) how pizza he can make
  (d) how could he make pizza

18. A: Do you want me to get that cake or the other one?

B: Both are great! You can have _____.

  (a) however you like
  (b) whichever you like
  (c) what else you like
  (d) no matter which you like

19. A: _____?

B: I think it's at the Rockstone Stadium in Greenleigh.

  (a) Where's the rock festival being held
  (b) Where's being held the rock festival
  (c) Where the rock festival is being held
  (d) Where the rock festival being held is

20. A: Robin says he'd be delighted _____ stay with us during summer vacation.

B: That's a relief! I thought he'd object.

  (a) if Ken coming to
  (b) Ken to come and
  (c) with Ken to come to
  (d) for Ken to come and

Part II **Questions 21—40**

Choose the best answer for the blank.

---

21. A common aphorism is "talking to _____ is the first sign of madness."

  (a) me
  (b) one
  (c) itself
  (d) oneself

22. When we receive a sudden shock, it can feel _____ our legs have turned to jelly.

  (a) like
  (b) though
  (c) as like
  (d) although

23. A large segment of the population agrees that wealthy people should pay more taxes to help _____.

  (a) poors
  (b) a poor
  (c) the poor
  (d) the poors

24. Although his hip-hop albums had been the fastest-selling in music history, after 2005 Eminem did not release another album _____ almost four years.

  (a) for
  (b) while
  (c) during
  (d) since

25. Academics are always interested to meet another professor _____ thesis topic is similar to their own.

(a) who
(b) who's
(c) which
(d) whose

26. _____, most parents still pay extra private tuition for their school-age children.

(a) As it is expensive
(b) It is as expensive
(c) As expensive it is
(d) As expensive as it is

27. Astronomy is complex, but kindergarten teachers should _____ Earth's position among the planets of our solar system.

(a) explain children enough to understand
(b) explain to understand children enough
(c) explain enough for children to understand
(d) enough explain for children to understand

28. It is generally agreed that nothing is _____ difficult as to foresee the future.

(a) so
(b) such
(c) so much
(d) such more

29. _____ baby sea turtles have emerged from their nests, they must reach the safety of the sea before being caught by a predator.

(a) Once
(b) If ever
(c) At once
(d) Whenever

30. Most people discover as they age that life is really _____ short and the years pass quickly.

(a) such
(b) much
(c) that
(d) very

31. According to school policy, teasing _____ and will be dealt with in the same way as bullying.

(a) will not allow
(b) is not allowed
(c) was not allowed
(d) is not being allowed

32. The injured man _____ to the hospital too late and was already dead on arrival.

(a) is brought
(b) has brought
(c) had brought
(d) had been brought

33. The Immigration Department wasn't _____ the refugees who were flooding into the remote offshore islands.

(a) aware
(b) aware of
(c) aware that
(d) aware of that

34. Although pressure is intense, no athlete can compete successfully if they miss too _____ training.

(a) many
(b) much
(c) a lot of
(d) many of

35. Pentax and Canon _____ new digital SLR models this month.

(a) brought out have both
(b) have both brought out
(c) brought out both have
(d) have brought both out

36. Italy is _____ known for the excellent quality of its coffee.

(a) well
(b) very
(c) such
(d) far

37. The trainee manager _____ at the presentation, but he had gone home early.

(a) would be
(b) should be
(c) is supposed to be
(d) was supposed to be

38. When a disagreement occurs, it is important to try to see things _____ the other person's point of view.

(a) after
(b) from
(c) through
(d) at

39. By the age of two the child _____ soundly through the night for over a year.

(a) has slept
(b) was sleeping
(c) has been sleeping
(d) had been sleeping

40. Audrey Hepburn had _____ sure sense of chic that she became a major fashion influence.

(a) so
(b) such
(c) such a
(d) a such

Part III **Questions 41—45**

Identify the option that contains an awkward expression or an error in grammar.

41 (a) A: I'm planning to conduct experiment on the psychological effects of being a prisoner.

(b) B: It would be better if you studied prison guards rather than prisoners.

(c) A: I've never thought of that before. Why?

(d) B: How to treat terrorists in prison is a big issue right now.

42. (a) A: What's up? You look really worried.

(b) B: I've just offered a promotion within my company.

(c) A: I would have thought that would be good news.

(d) B: Maybe. But it means I'd have to move from Seoul to Pyeongtaek.

43. (a) A: I'd like to confirm my reservation for next week.

(b) B: Can you give me your name and reservation number, please?

(c) A: It's Ken Brown, AH09-821. You do have my reservation, don't you?

(d) B: Yes, Mr. Brown. We have you reserved for March 6 through 8 a non-smoking double room.

44. (a) A: I've just spent a few days with my relatives in Seoul.

(b) B: Did you enjoy being in our capital city?

(c) A: I always enjoy visiting Seoul, and I wouldn't like to live there because it's too big.

(d) B: I love the sea, which is why I prefer living in Busan.

45. (a) A: How did you like the show you went to last night?

(b) B: It was much too long. It lasted until 11 o'clock.

(c) A: Was Dr. Laugh as humorous as people have been saying?

(d) B: I didn't find him funny at all. In fact, I was embarrassing for him.

Part IV Questions 46—50

Identify the option that contains an awkward expression or an error in grammar.

46. (a) At Harvard University, 55,000 mice and 1,500 primates are kept for animal experimentation. (b) The vast majority of the mice are used in programs focusing on genetic research. (c) Scientists are always aware that a stray bacteria could wipe out millions of dollars worth of animal experiments. (d) Therefore, instead researchers want to enter the laboratories, they have to shower and change into scrubs.

47. (a) My mother, whom we hope will be out of the hospital soon, is looking forward to being home again. (b) She had brain surgery two weeks ago. (c) The doctors say that she will take two months to fully recover. (d) However, my mother is hoping to be able to return to work in about six weeks.

48. (a) The Ishtar Gate, dedicated to the goddess Ishtar, was one of the gates of the ancient city of Babylon. (b) King Nebuchadnezzar II was constructed it in about 575 BC. (c) For many centuries, the gate was considered one of the Seven Wonders of the World. (d) The walls surrounding the doors were covered in blue-glazed tiles with gold animals in bas-relief.

49. (a) Greenwich Mean Time (GMT) was established when the Royal Observatory was built in Greenwich, London, in 1685, to help establish longitude at sea. (b) More recently, the advent of atomic clocks has ushered in a new time system, Coordinated Universal Time or UTC. (c) Some countries have retained GMT, but the majority doesn't use it any longer, preferring UTC. (d) However, many newspapers and television channels fail to distinguish between GMT and UTC.

50. (a) The term misogyny was coined by Greek philosophers to describe women-haters. (b) The parallel term is misandry, which is hatred of the male sex. (c) Both terms are related to misanthropy, which is hatred of humanity in general. (d) The Greek philosophers considered misogyny to be caused by gynophobia—that is, fear of women.

This is the end of the Grammar section. Do NOT move on to the next section until instructed to do so. You are NOT allowed to turn to any other section of the test.

TEPS

VOCABULARY

DIRECTIONS

This part of the exam tests your vocabulary skills. You will have 15 minutes to complete the 50 questions. Be sure to follow the directions given by the proctor.

Part I **Questions 1—25**

Choose the best answer for the blank.

1. A: You don't look very happy. What's up?
   B: This kind of music always _____ me sad.

   (a) hands
   (b) feels
   (c) makes
   (d) gives

2. A: I'd better be going.
   B: OK, let's _____ over the weekend.

   (a) call out
   (b) talk it up
   (c) touch down
   (d) get in touch

3. A: I'm looking for a new lawyer. Who do you go to?
   B: Lia Cheng, but she's so busy she's not taking new _____ right now.

   (a) clients
   (b) consumers
   (c) agents
   (d) partners

4. A: Could his story really be true?
   B: I don't think so. We should probably _____ the facts before accepting it.

   (a) tug
   (b) check
   (c) leave
   (d) put

5. A: Congratulations on your pregnancy! How are you holding up?
   B: Unfortunately, I'm feeling really _____.

   (a) electric
   (b) elated
   (c) naughty
   (d) nauseous

6. A: The subprime mortgage crisis has had serious consequences.
   B: That's right. Many homeowners have been badly _____.

   (a) affected
   (b) effected
   (c) infected
   (d) defected

7. A: My boyfriend's never going to come back to me!
   B: I'm sorry, but I think you have to _____ the situation.

   (a) except
   (b) accept
   (c) harass
   (d) receive

8. A: I heard that most of the first-class passengers died in the accident.
   B: The front of the plane took the full _____ of the crash.

   (a) brutality
   (b) implosion
   (c) impact
   (d) absorption

9. A: The Phillies are a much better team than the Dodgers.

    B: On what _____ did you make that decision?

    (a) bases
    (b) base
    (c) basics
    (d) basis

10. A: Visiting my sister always makes me question whether I want to have children.

    B: Me, too. Her kids are so _____.

    (a) unruly
    (b) unfavorable
    (c) unfamiliar
    (d) uncoordinated

11. A: I heard your aunt was injured at the supermarket.

    B: Yes, someone ran their shopping _____ into her and knocked her down.

    (a) cart
    (b) bag
    (c) basket
    (d) buggy

12. A: What's your cousin Moira like?

    B: She's great! But she _____ money like water.

    (a) runs up
    (b) runs out of
    (c) goes at
    (d) goes through

13. A: My favorite poem is *The Road Less Traveled* by Robert Frost.

    B: I hate that poem! We _____ it to death when I was in high school.

    (a) watched
    (b) analyzed
    (c) resolved
    (d) clarified

14. A: I took my diamond earrings to the jewelers to be _____.

    B: Good idea. Your insurance company will be happy about that.

    (a) pattered
    (b) appraised
    (c) appreciated
    (d) depreciated

15. A: Can you tell me the way to the post office?

    B: Sure. Drive through the _____, turn right by the gas station, and go one more block.

    (a) intersection
    (b) shoulder
    (c) freeway
    (d) avenue

16. A: I owe you an _____ for my behavior last night.

    B: Don't worry about it. It's not important.

    (a) apology
    (b) excuse
    (c) offense
    (d) admission

17. A: Your new colleague had a great time at the party last night.

B: Yes, Rod is very _____.

(a) extreme
(b) excited
(c) existent
(d) extroverted

18. A: You look really sick! Go and see a doctor.

B: You're right, and I'll have to _____ my reservation for tonight's dinner.

(a) bracket
(b) defuse
(c) predict
(d) cancel

19. A: How did your dad react when you told him about the car?

B: He was really _____ with me, I can tell you!

(a) raging
(b) dubious
(c) furious
(d) maddening

20. A: What happened to that case you were working on last month?

B: The wife will _____ trial, charged with murdering her husband.

(a) stand
(b) undergo
(c) experience
(d) withstand

21. A: How was your exam?

B: Awful. By the time I finished I felt _____.

(a) devastated
(b) scattered
(c) splintered
(d) injured

22. A: You look really tired.

B: I feel it. I didn't sleep a _____ last night.

(a) beat
(b) breath
(c) nod
(d) wink

23. A: I won a free holiday in Bermuda!

B: Wow! Does that include airfare and _____?

(a) reserve
(b) accommodation
(c) service
(d) confirmation

24. A: I heard your aunt broke her leg. How is she doing?

B: She was _____ from the hospital this morning.

(a) rushed
(b) admitted
(c) discharged
(d) disbursed

25. A: How do you manage to get straight As on your homework assignments?

B: Well, one thing I always do is a spell _____.

(a) check
(b) tally
(c) routine
(d) checklist

Choose the best answer for the blank.

26. Famous musicians generally spend hours _____ with the orchestra before their concerts.

    (a) conforming
    (b) straddling
    (c) rehearsing
    (d) executing

27. Queen Victoria _____ longer than any other British monarch.

    (a) resigned
    (b) reigned
    (c) registered
    (d) reinstated

28. Many Britney Spears fans have been severely _____ by the controversies surrounding her personal life.

    (a) disillusioned
    (b) reprimanded
    (c) damaged
    (d) accused

29. All our orders are _____ within two days, or you can upgrade to one day for only $3.99 extra.

    (a) generated
    (b) fulfilled
    (c) infected
    (d) shipped

30. When *Vogue* (UK) was _____ in 1912 it made history by being the first overseas edition of a US magazine.

    (a) floated
    (b) proposed
    (c) publicized
    (d) launched

31. The drop in mortgage _____ rates for homeowners is one of the few benefits of the present economic crisis.

    (a) interest
    (b) money
    (c) currency
    (d) wallet

32. The novelist Ernest Hemingway _____ himself in the cultures of the places he visited before writing vividly about them.

    (a) surrounded
    (b) riveted
    (c) concentrated
    (d) immersed

33. Since 1988, when the Kawerau Bridge became the world's first full-time bungee site, it has been _____ as the home of bungee jumping.

    (a) collected
    (b) recognized
    (c) inspired
    (d) varnished

34. Cyclists will be able to bike close to the North Korean border when a restricted military area is opened to _____ later this year.

    (a) personnel
    (b) commoners
    (c) civilians
    (d) wheelers

35. She sought a divorce from her pop-star husband _____ cruelty.

    (a) on the grounds of
    (b) in accordance with
    (c) with the antecedent of
    (d) on suspicion of

36. The music of Norah Jones _____ jazz, soul, and mellow pop to create a celebrated, award-winning sound.

    (a) crosses
    (b) smoothes
    (c) blends
    (d) slices

37. Eco Villages represent a worldwide movement to create _____ developments which do not harm the environment in any way.

    (a) coherent
    (b) sustainable
    (c) systemic
    (d) malign

38. We _____ our chef's special: fresh rainbow trout with pesto sauce and spring vegetables.

    (a) refer
    (b) mention
    (c) recommend
    (d) explain

39. Each year our company _____ a few talented graduates from throughout the country.

    (a) searches
    (b) deducts
    (c) subscribes
    (d) recruits

40. The Department of Health recommends that people over 40 years old have their blood pressure _____ regularly.

    (a) checked
    (b) determined
    (c) controlled
    (d) audited

41. The trade union is concerned that many workers do not have a written _____.

    (a) scandal
    (b) negotiation
    (c) stipulation
    (d) contract

42. When Adolf Hitler became the leader of Germany in 1933, he _____ democracy and behaved like a dictator.

    (a) abolished
    (b) unhinged
    (c) vetoed
    (d) revised

43. The global economic crisis has led to workers in many countries being fired or _____.

    (a) let up
    (b) laid off
    (c) given up
    (d) left off

44. Whenever Maria gets excited she _____ wildly with her hands while talking.

    (a) impresses
    (b) dilates
    (c) communicates
    (d) gesticulates

45. This week Apple warned that iPhone and iPod users could receive small electric shocks while using these products, due to the buildup of _____ electricity in dry weather.

(a) timid
(b) negative
(c) static
(d) menial

46. China fears that the Dalai Lama visits foreign countries in order to _____ Tibetan independence from China.

(a) elevate
(b) inhibit
(c) traverse
(d) promote

47. Please try to _____ as much of the packaging that comes into your home as you can.

(a) recycle
(b) escalate
(c) convert
(d) reprocess

48. Gossip seems harmless, but is in fact so _____ that it can destroy friendships.

(a) insidious
(b) invidious
(c) surreptitious
(d) disingenuous

49. Throughout the world, the multinational company found _____ politicians whom they were able to bribe easily.

(a) debauched
(b) defiled
(c) crooked
(d) perverted

50. Medical practitioners are concerned because many bacterial diseases are becoming _____ to antibiotic drugs.

(a) unyielding
(b) resistant
(c) antagonistic
(d) repellent

This is the end of the Vocabulary section. Do NOT move on to the Reading Comprehension section until instructed to do so. You are NOT allowed to turn to any other section of the test.

READING COMPREHENSION

Part I **Questions 1—16**

Read the passage. Then choose the option that best completes the passage.

---

1. Newtown Aquatic Center is open every day from 6:00 am to 9:00 pm. It offers a full range of water-related activities under one roof. The Aquatic Center features a 50-meter main pool, a competitive diving pool, learners' and toddlers' pools, plus private spas, saunas, a swim shop, cafe, and short-term daycare. Activities include kayaking, water polo, underwater hockey, and aqua jogging. In addition, you can rest assured that _____, so chlorine-induced eye and breathing problems are a thing of the past.

    (a) all pool water is carefully monitored
    (b) children are not allowed in the pools
    (c) patrons can release stress in the pools
    (d) the water filters are covered properly

2.

> To the Editor,
>
> The issue of human rights abuses by United States interrogators is crucial to international attitudes about the US, which would be well advised to learn from its own history. During World War II, interrogators were trained to extract information through psychological and not physical means. Prisoners of war were well treated, but their conversations were wiretapped and subsequently studied carefully. Reports on prisoners' idle chatter were found to be a rich source of useful intelligence. If the US is really interested in building new nation-states in Iraq and Afghanistan, then it should remember the Golden Rule and apply it when _____.

    (a) writing reports on prisoner interrogations
    (b) POWs' conversations are being examined
    (c) cross-examining accused terrorists in court
    (d) formulating and implementing an interrogation policy

3. Researchers have discovered that mockingbirds can recognize people who have touched their nests in the past. Zoology researchers at the University of Florida made this unexpected discovery during a study of the effects of urbanization on mockingbirds. Birds are much more aware of all aspects of their environment than previously thought, and humans are an important part of that environment. As part of mockingbirds' survival strategies, they have learned to identify people _____.

(a) who have a natural antipathy to birds
(b) who have previously threatened their nests
(c) who form an irregular part of their ecosystem
(d) who look significantly different from each other

4. Although this is a golden age for Spanish men's tennis, it has been nine years since a Spanish woman reached the singles semifinals of a Grand Slam event. However, a short but sturdy 20-year-old shows promise of reaching No. 1 in the world. Carla Suarez has a powerful one-handed backhand that makes her a challenging and complex player. Suarez has spent considerable time studying Justine Henin, _____.

(a) who taught her to tee off
(b) a powerful women's volleyball finalist
(c) who is also a sports journalist
(d) from whom she learned her backhand

5. The Internet's potential as an agent of social change is being demonstrated in China. Incidents involving individual citizens and powerful Communist Party officials used to be known only to nearby residents. But now such cases are being broadcast on the Internet, and millions of people are staging what is becoming known as "online mass incidents." Public awareness of democratic ideas such as accountability and transparency is growing. With each case _____, progress is inching forward.

(a) defended by the local bureaucracy
(b) that is censored by local officials
(c) that is successfully fought on the web
(d) shown to be invalid by the government

6. Recent research into business leadership reveals surprising results. Traits like being a good listener, a good team builder, or an able communicator do not seem to be very important for leading a successful company. What matters is emotional stability, conscientiousness, reliability, attention to detail, and persistence. CEOs need to fill an organizational role, not a charismatic one. Warm, flexible, empathetic people are less likely to succeed as business leaders than _____.

   (a) flamboyant, enthusiastic, truly idealistic types
   (b) charming, ruthless, essentially callous leaders
   (c) resolute, efficient, slightly boring personalities
   (d) magnetic, larger-than-life, very engaging characters

7. Godwit Air is way ahead when it comes to passenger facilities! All our airplanes boast three innovative features. We are the first airline in the world to install discrete face screens between you and the next person, which can be activated at your convenience. Our planes boast more bathrooms per passenger than regulations demand. And our new headsets not only deliver superior stereo sound, but _____.

   (a) with entertainment options
   (b) keep exterior sounds out, too
   (c) when you want to sleep in comfort
   (d) with its selection of meals

8. The Irish have celebrated St. Patrick's Day, March 17, as a religious holiday for over one thousand years. When Irish immigrants flooded into the US during the Irish potato famine of the 1840s, the newspapers lampooned the St. Patrick's Day parades in cartoons. However, the Irish soon realized that, in spite of their poverty and lack of education, their great numbers gave them political power. They began to organize themselves into a power bloc known as the "green machine." Soon, St. Patrick's Day Parades became a show of strength attended by _____.

   (a) Irish immigrants fresh off the boat
   (b) environmentally conscious Irish workers
   (c) political candidates hoping to woo the Irish
   (d) Socialist parties seeking support from the left

9. Major airplane crashes are dramatic and command the attention of the world's media. This creates _____. Nevertheless, statistics show a different picture. In the last 20 years there have been 2,100 commercial airline accidents. However, this is set in the context of 11.5 billion passenger trips. The chances of surviving an air flight are 99.9999%.

(a) many photos of wrecked planes
(b) a dramatic illustration of how safe it is
(c) some people to suffer from aviophobia
(d) a perception that air transport is inherently risky

10. Black holes in space are areas into which light waves are drawn and cannot escape. Recently, Israeli scientists succeeded in creating a sonic black hole, trapping sound waves instead of light. The aim of the experiment was to discover more about how the universe works. This could help physicists to _____. It will also give a new perspective on some complex issues involving quantum mechanics, thermodynamics, and gravity.

(a) learn more about naturally occurring black holes
(b) reduce sound levels in particularly noisy locations
(c) prove definitively that Israeli scientists were correct
(d) test whether the experiment is possible or not

11. The levels and variety of media exposure in children's lives are topics receiving increasing attention in academic circles. It has been found that media can encourage violence, but it can also stimulate pro-social behavior. However, because of the swift rate of technological development, _____. So the question still remains, are children at risk in our media-rich society?

(a) children are not influenced by any single medium for very long
(b) the general public knows the potential effects of media on children
(c) many parents can assess the programs to which their children are exposed
(d) there is a lack of data on the long-term effects of new media forms on children's behavior

12. The Museum of Modern Art (MoMA), in New York City, has played a unique role in developing and collecting modernist art. It is generally agreed to _____. Scholars come not just to view MoMA's unparalleled collections, but also to study the history of modern and contemporary art in the museum's extensive archives. MoMA was the brainchild of Abby Rockefeller and opened in 1929, nine days after the Wall Street Crash.

(a) rival the Louvre in its extensive acquisitions
(b) contain many valuable examples of classical artworks
(c) be a unique showcase of ancient indigenous painting
(d) be the most influential museum of modern art in the world

13. Homework is _____. However, studies of homework have repeatedly highlighted its negative effects. Physical and emotional fatigue, satiation, and lack of time for leisure and community activities are consistently reported. Cheating is also a problem, through copying from other students, or through having a tutor help with homework assignments. Studies of elementary school students show no difference in achievement later in life between students who received homework and those who did not.

(a) exhausting for students
(b) a path to success in life
(c) a cornerstone of education
(d) understood to create problems

14. A new study conducted at the School of Veterinary Medicine in Barcelona, Spain, suggests that the innocent-looking English cocker spaniel may be one of the world's most aggressive dogs. Cocker spaniels were found to be more likely than other dogs to behave aggressively towards their owners, as well as unfamiliar people. In contrast, dogs from other aggressive breeds were more likely to show hostility towards other dogs. The study adds to increasing evidence indicating that aggressiveness is caused not so much by environment as by _____.

(a) lack of training during puppyhood
(b) genetically inherited characteristics
(c) the temperaments of the dogs' owners
(d) the geographic origins of various canine breeds

15. The Depression-era robbers Bonnie and Clyde have become celebrated American antiheroes. _____, the truth is that they were bumbling and utterly ruthless murderers. After they were gunned down by police in 1934, Bonnie and Clyde were almost forgotten for thirty years. The fame they enjoy today is solely due to the 1967 movie *Bonnie and Clyde*, which portrayed them as glamorous, dashing, polite, and persecuted. The many recent biographies written about the couple attest to a continuing fascination with their lives.

(a) Moreover
(b) However
(c) Therefore
(d) Likewise

16. Welcome to the 4th Annual East Asian English Conference. Since the East Asian English Society was founded in 2005, our conferences have gained a reputation for a uniquely harmonious sharing of research and resources among English teachers of the East Asian region. _____, several EAES task forces are now tackling the biggest issues facing English teachers in the area. This year sees our biggest conference yet, with almost 1,000 attendees gathered here in the lovely historic city of Kyoto.

(a) And yet
(b) In the end
(c) As a result
(d) By contrast

Part II **Questions 17—37**

Read the passage and the question. Then choose the option that best answers the question.

17. A recent article in the journal *Sleep Medicine* reports that people who sleep too little, not enough, or erratically are at higher risk of developing diabetes. Other recent studies have also shown a link between length of sleep and obesity, heart disease, and premature death. It appears that sleep disruption affects hormones and proteins which regulate appetite and plays a role in various chronic diseases.

Q: What is the best title for the passage?
(a) Sleep Patterns Impact Health
(b) Insomnia Implicated in Illness
(c) Diabetes Caused by Irregular Sleep
(d) Sleeping Patterns and Body Weight

18. Discussions about semantics, syntax, and phonology focus on abstract concepts and generally use constructed examples. Little attention is paid to such factors as who is speaking and the interrelationships between language and life. Dissecting language in isolation is a limited and arbitrary approach. Instead, it is imperative to study the language of real people in the real world.

Q: What is the main idea of the passage?
(a) Social factors must be included in any study of linguistics.
(b) Linguistic abstractions are useless when studying human language.
(c) Natural utterances should be used when constructing language theory.
(d) Linguistics should be broadened to include other areas of specialization.

19. Victorian literature refers to British literature written during the reign of Queen Victoria (1837-1901). During the 19th century the novel became the leading form of literature in English, and this period is often regarded as the peak of British, American, Russian, and French literature. Victorian novels contained many detailed descriptions of the effects of rapid industrialization on the lives of the working poor and were powerful agents of social change. As the century progressed, novels became grimmer and more realistic, with unhappy endings seen more frequently.

Q: What is the passage mainly about?
(a) Popularity of 19th-century literature
(b) Social realism in the Victorian novel
(c) The characteristics of Victorian literature
(d) The rise of the English novel during the 1800s

20. This year the spring 'Hi Seoul Festival' runs from May 1 through May 9. As always during the festival, the city's cultural venues will feature the talents of artists from many different countries. However, this year the Seoul city government is placing its main emphasis not on culture, but on the environment. The many free activities will include bikes at subway stations throughout Jongno, whole streets closed to cars to permit safe cycling, children's craft activities which find new uses for common packaging materials, and street theater groups demonstrating how to better care for Seoul's environment.

Q: What is the announcement mainly about?
(a) 'Green' activities in Seoul
(b) Children's activities during a festival
(c) The new focus of the Hi Seoul Festival
(d) Cultural events during the Hi Seoul Festival

21. At the East Asian World Economic Forum, the twin issues of the global economy and environmental threats were discussed. Asian cities are vulnerable to the impact of climate change, as many are situated on coastlines, and two thirds of the world's poorest people live in Asia. It was emphasized that these two issues cannot be separated, and a comprehensive policy response must be adopted. Designing low-carbon economies and creating jobs through green growth plans were discussed.

Q: Which of the following is correct according to the article?
(a) Green policies restrict growth in the job market.
(b) Extreme weather conditions could affect many Asian cities.
(c) Asia has the opportunity to lead the world in environmental issues.
(d) Climate change is a bigger problem than the world economic crisis.

22. The term "propaganda" was first used in 1622 by Pope Gregory VI, who established a society for "Propagating the Faith." In 1933, Hitler realized the potential of propaganda, creating a new position, Minister of Propaganda, for Joseph Goebbels, who was very effective in this post. Some key propaganda techniques that have been identified include: denigrating opponents, appealing to the emotions rather than to reason, emphasizing the importance of joining the group, and building a highly biased case.

Q: What is the best title for this passage?
(a) Propaganda Techniques
(b) Propaganda: An Overview
(c) The Origins of Propaganda
(d) Propaganda in Totalitarian Regimes

23. Saint Benedict is revered as the father of western monasticism, but very few facts are known about his life. The only definitive date is a visit paid him by the Gothic king Totila around 542. Benedict lived at a time of great social change, when Imperial Rome was sacked by the Goths, emptied of inhabitants, and then transformed into the Rome of the medieval papacy. Although Benedict's reforming zeal was at first resisted—at least one attempt was made to poison him—his wise and balanced monastic rule became the norm throughout Europe and has also provided inspiration for many secular legislators.

Q: Which of the following is correct according to the article?
(a) Benedict was an influence on law creators.
(b) Many legends arose about Benedict's life.
(c) The king of the Goths threatened Benedict's life.
(d) Benedict was responsible for Rome's transformation.

24. Until the Beijing Olympics, South Korea had won every Olympic gold medal in women's archery since 1984. At the Beijing Olympics, the US coach Lee Ki Sik, also a Korean, was reported as saying that the Korean women were unbeatable. "It's like they are adults shooting with elementary school children." During the 2004 Athens Olympics, the Korean women's team broke three world records during the initial ranking rounds. So the winning of a silver medal in the women's individual event in Beijing was a cause for mourning, rather than rejoicing, in South Korea.

Q: Which of the following is correct according to the article?
(a) Women's archery became an Olympic sport in 1984.
(b) The US coach criticized the South Korean archery team.
(c) South Korea leads the world in both men's and women's archery.
(d) The Korean women's archery team did not meet expectations in Beijing.

25. No other jazz musician has had as strong an influence on rock music as Miles Davis. He played a crucial role in every development in jazz from the 1940s until his death in 1991. As a trumpeter, he was not technically perfect, but made up for this with his unique tone and phrasing. His quintets became the most important jazz group of the 1950s and 1960s. In 1968, he began experimenting with a fusion of jazz and rock. Towards the end of his life, he surrounded himself with young musicians, and his work became increasingly commercial. The critics complained, but his concerts sold out all over the world.

Q: Which of the following is correct about Miles Davis?
(a) He gave up jazz for rock music.
(b) He was famous for his precision with the trumpet.
(c) As he grew older, he lost touch with his audience.
(d) He played in quintets in the 50s.

26. The Rose International School is pleased to announce the opening of our Early Bird program for children aged 3-5 years old. There are two certified teachers in every Early Bird classroom. Children learn through play and exploration in which different learning styles and intelligence levels are catered to. We aim not only at academic but also personal development and foster the skills and attitudes that will lead to a lifelong love of learning. Please find contact information below.

Q: Which of the following is correct according to the advertisement?
(a) The focus is on academic success.
(b) The school is involved in formal learning only.
(c) The school teaches children how to be independent learners.
(d) The program accommodates children who learn in different ways.

27. Crete, a large island lying in the Mediterranean between Greece and Turkey, is generally considered to be the oldest civilization in Europe. During the Bronze Age it was the center of the Minoan civilization, which existed over 4,000 years ago. It came to an end around 1450 BC, possibly because of a natural catastrophe. At a time when people in most other European countries were living in caves, Crete had both a written language and a plumbing system. Homer's *Odyssey* says that Crete was densely populated, with ninety cities.

Q: Which of the following is correct according to the passage?
(a) Crete was destroyed in 1450 BC.
(b) The Minoans were a primitive Stone Age culture.
(c) The Minoans had their own plumbing system.
(d) Crete had a higher population during Homer's time than it does now.

28. Elder abuse is becoming recognized as a problem in many societies. It is defined as doing something, or failing to do something, which results in harm to an elderly person. It includes physical, sexual, or emotional abuse; neglecting or deserting an older person for whom you are responsible; and taking or misusing an elderly person's money or property. Elder abuse can happen in the family, in hospitals, or in nursing homes. Many forms of elder abuse are recognized as domestic or family violence.

Q: Which of the following is correct according to the passage?
(a) Elderly people are mainly abused by other elderly people.
(b) Elder abuse includes the theft of personal belongings.
(c) Old people are most at risk with people unknown to them.
(d) Senior citizens are at risk from criminal activity such as muggings.

29. Van Gogh's dramatic life story is well known, especially the fact that his right ear was cut off. It has generally been supposed that Van Gogh cut off his own ear in a fit of madness. However, recently two art historians have suggested that Van Gogh's ear was accidentally cut off by his friend, the painter Gauguin, with his sword during an argument. They posit that Van Gogh told people he cut off the ear himself to protect his friend. Whatever the truth is, Gauguin left Arles and never saw Van Gogh again, who was hospitalized and in a critical state for several days.

Q: Which of the following is correct according to the passage?
(a) Van Gogh cut off his own ear.
(b) Van Gogh and Gauguin argued about their art.
(c) Gauguin may have inadvertently cut off Van Gogh's ear.
(d) The painters' friendship was not affected by the incident.

30.

To the Householder

The City Council has decided, after two years of research and planning, to make Orchard City a model of an environmentally sustainable community. The new City Plan includes massive tree planting schemes, designated bike trails throughout the city and environs, updated recycling facilities, and tougher controls on industrial pollution. In order to fund these new policies, the City Council will increase property taxes by 5% beginning September 1. These proposals will inevitably cause a rise in home values as Orchard City becomes a sought-after locality, so homeowners have much to gain, both financially and in terms of quality of life.

Q: Why did the City Council write this letter?
(a) To get householders' support for the new policies
(b) To tell citizens that their properties will increase in price
(c) To inform home owners that taxes are going to increase
(d) To persuade residents to become environmentally aware

31. Scientists from the University of Central Florida say they have developed cancer tests that could be sold over the counter. The tests could detect seven to ten different kinds of common cancer from one drop of blood in only a few minutes. In contrast, existing methods of testing are expensive, require a lot of blood, take several hours, and can only detect advanced cancers. The new cancer tests are based on nanotechnology, which uses microscopic materials.

Q: Which of the following is correct according to the article?
(a) The new cancer tests have already begun to sell.
(b) Over-the-counter cancer tests are proving successful.
(c) Most kinds of cancer can be detected with the new tests.
(d) The new tests are possible because of different technology.

32. A study of women in Michigan has found that what your mother ate during pregnancy can have a significant effect on your weight gain as an adult. Lake Michigan is known to have large amounts of industrial pollutants in the water. It was found that mothers who had eaten the most DDT (dichloro-diphenyl-trichloro-ethane) contaminated fish had daughters who were 20 pounds heavier by the age of 30. Fatty fish like tuna and salmon contain lots of DDT. Guidelines recommend eating no more than two servings of fish a week from certain lakes and rivers, and pregnant women should eat less.

Q: Which of the following is correct according to the article?
(a) Pregnant women should not eat fish.
(b) Eating tuna and salmon cannot harm your health.
(c) Conditions in the womb can have health effects in adulthood.
(d) The Michigan area was studied because fishing is popular there.

33. The road to modern video games is paved with all kinds of intriguing innovations that didn't quite catch on. However, we wouldn't have the best-selling, role-playing games of today without the persistent, risk-taking engineers and inventors of past decades. For example, the VHS video game Action Max from the toy company Worlds of Wonder necessitated a VCR and was non-interactive: the game was the same each time. But when Worlds of Wonder collapsed, many of its engineers are said to have taken jobs at the more successful Nintendo.

Q: What can be inferred from the article?
(a) Older video game technologies are now regarded as irrelevant.
(b) Lessons learned from the Worlds of Wonder failure were used at Nintendo.
(c) VHS game engineers were not able to develop more sophisticated games.
(d) The technological superiority of Nintendo led to the collapse of Worlds of Wonder.

34. As technology changes the nature of work and even eliminates some categories of jobs, many American colleges are starting to overhaul their curricula to better prepare students to join 21st-century workforces. New programs are being constructed to offer relevant coursework and skills. These new programs include courses in business ethics, online education, homeland security, biofuels, and sustainable technology. Armed with knowledge in these subject areas, American graduates should have an easier time finding jobs than they did previously, when general liberal-arts expertise was all they had to offer.

Q: What can be inferred about current American college programs?
(a) They focus solely on liberal arts courses.
(b) They are not meeting the demands of employers.
(c) They are experiencing a drop in student enrollment.
(d) They avoid subjects such as biofuels and online education.

35. A new community in Germany, Vauban, is conducting a social experiment in car-free living. Street parking, garages, and driveways are forbidden and cars must be parked in a large garage on the edge of the suburb. As a result, 70% of families in Vauban do not own a car. The experiment is part of "smart planning," a growing movement in Europe to curb greenhouse gas emissions, of which 12% is caused by cars. Suburbs have traditionally been designed around car use, but urban planners around the globe are starting to make them more compact, with better access to public transport and stores and less space for parking.

Q: What can be inferred from the passage?
(a) Urban planners in Europe are trying to phase out private cars.
(b) Germany is at the forefront of environmentally friendly living.
(c) Vauban will fail as an experiment in car-free urban life.
(d) Many European communities are designed on "smart planning" principles.

36. A new genetic study proposes that birds originated 100 million years ago, during the time that dinosaurs ruled the earth. Until now, studies based on fossil records dated the origin of birds to 66 million years ago, about the time that dinosaurs became extinct. However, geneticists argue that the true origin of a species happens when a genetic line splits. For example, molecular biologists now say that fowl, like chickens, and waterfowl, like ducks, split 90 million years ago to form different kinds of birds. The new findings, based on DNA synthesis, may replace fossil specimens as the most exact method of dating species.

Q: What can be inferred from the passage?
(a) All birds are descended from chickens.
(b) Waterfowl and fowl are not actually related.
(c) Fossils accurately record the origin of a species.
(d) Geneticists believe birds coexisted with dinosaurs.

37. Jimmy Carter was President of the United States from 1977 to 1981, but his presidency finished amid widespread criticism of his policies. However, since his term of office ended, Carter has become renowned for his international humanitarian work. Carter and his wife Rosalynn established the Carter Center, which conducts peace negotiations, has monitored 70 elections in 28 countries, and works towards disease eradication and prevention in the developing world. Carter is also a key figure in Habitat for Humanity and received the Nobel Peace Prize in 2002.

Q: What can be inferred about Jimmy Carter?
(a) He is highly respected for his achievements while President.
(b) He sought to redeem his presidency through his charity work.
(c) He used his position as ex-President to influence other governments.
(d) He received the Nobel Peace Prize for his work with Habitat for Humanity.

Part III Questions 38—40

Read the passage. Then identify the option that does NOT belong.

38. Cancer Research UK reports that skin cancer is increasing faster than any other disease in the UK. (a) It is predicted that by 2024 the disease will be the fourth most common form of cancer in Britain. (b) Women are more likely to go to the doctor and be diagnosed as having skin cancer, but more men die from the disease. (c) Experts say that artificial tanning is contributing to the rise of skin cancer. (d) Therefore, some people think the government should put a tax on sun beds.

39. The Cambodian government may open the Angkor Wat temples at night to attract more tourists. (a) This is to attract more tourists and therefore more income for this impoverished country. (b) Already, around 500,000 tourists are expected to visit Angkor Wat this year. (c) In 2003 there were riots when a rumor spread that a Thai actress had claimed Angkor Wat was in Thailand. (d) But conservationists are unhappy about the prospect of increased tourism, saying that the earth beneath the temple is already being destabilized.

40. Generation Y is a term used to describe the generation born between the late seventies and early nineties. (a) They are characterized by their habitual use of the Internet, computers, MP3s, and mobile phones. (b) In addition, they are generally highly skilled at multi-tasking. (c) Gen Yers differ from those of previous generations in their tendency to have positive relationships with their parents, to whom they talk on a wide range of topics. (d) Young people in China experience a wide generation gap with their parents.

This is the end of the Reading Comprehension section. Please remain seated until the proctor has instructed otherwise. You are NOT allowed to turn to any other section of the test.

Actual Test 1

1

M Do you know when the meeting's been rescheduled for?

W _____

(a) Sure, see you there.
(b) I don't have time now.
(c) We'll be discussing our sales.
(d) It's been moved to after lunch.

2

W I can't concentrate. My back is killing me!

M _____

(a) I know, isn't it great?
(b) You should see a doctor.
(c) Thanks, I think I've recovered.
(d) Frankly, I can't figure it out either.

3

W How did you get to the post office?

M _____

(a) By city bus.
(b) Ship it express.
(c) I used to work there.
(d) It should be open now.

4

W I don't get why I haven't been promoted yet.

M _____

(a) Congratulations!
(b) Really? Let me try.
(c) He hasn't gotten here yet.
(d) The company's hiring from outside.

5

M Do you have our client's contact number?

W _____

(a) You can use my cell.
(b) She didn't provide one.
(c) Make sure to call all the clients.
(d) The phone's been ringing off the hook.

6

M Can I ask a favor?

W _____

(a) I'll ask again later.
(b) Anything you need.
(c) No, I don't have one.
(d) Please answer the phone.

7

M How have you been, Rebecca? It's been a while.

W _____

(a) I haven't seen her in ages.
(b) Hold on. Let me get her for you.
(c) Thank you. It's nice to meet you, too.
(d) Just fine, thanks for asking. And you?

8

W Mr. Kane isn't in. Can I take a message?

M _____

(a) He and I go way back.
(b) Do I have any messages?
(c) Tell him I'll call back later.
(d) Yes, put him through, please.

9

M I'm so embarrassed I missed my flight!

W _____

(a) From gate 42.
(b) I hate waiting in airports.
(c) I'm sure you can rebook it.
(d) It arrives in Pittsburgh tomorrow.

10

W This is our most popular printer model.

M _____

(a) How many would you like to order?
(b) Thanks, but I'm set on a cheaper one.
(c) What seems to be the problem with it?
(d) I need four printouts in black and white.

11

W All employees need to stay until 5:30 today.

M _____

(a) I'm not wearing a watch.
(b) Will we be paid overtime?
(c) Great. I'll see you at 8:30 tomorrow.
(d) I think they're in the conference room.

12

W What do you think of the new boss?

M _____

(a) I like this company.
(b) Please, call me Bill.
(c) He has a lot of good ideas.
(d) He's arriving this afternoon.

13

M Sorry! I can't believe I spilled my coffee on you!

W _____

(a) My suit is at the cleaners.
(b) Don't worry. It was only a few drops.
(c) Sure, I'll have one with cream and sugar.
(d) Just let me know when you've made the copies.

14

W I love how you've redecorated your living room.

M _____

(a) There's plenty of room!
(b) Thanks, I'm glad you like it.
(c) Sure, let's sit down and relax.
(d) Move the couch against the wall.

15

M Are you bringing anyone to the party tonight?

W _____

(a) I'm happy to be invited.
(b) Maybe a couple of my friends.
(c) I'll definitely be there.
(d) It was so much fun, wasn't it?

16

W When are we getting together for dinner?
M I'm free this Thursday.
W Sorry, I have plans. What about Friday?
M _____

(a) I really enjoyed it.
(b) They can go together.
(c) Yes, I think that'll work.
(d) You can relax over the weekend.

17

M Ms. Williams, you have a call on line 2.
W Did they give you a name?
M Yes, it's Mr. John Lee.
W _____

(a) May I borrow your phone book?
(b) Great. I've been expecting his call.
(c) It's very nice to meet you, Mr. Lee.
(d) Sorry, he's on the other line right now.

18

W Where's the nearest pharmacy?

M There's one at the end of the block.

W On the right or the left?

M _____

(a) To pick up my prescription.

(b) You should ask at the pharmacy.

(c) There's a 30-story office building.

(d) It's across from the doughnut shop.

19

W How do you like your coffee?

M With extra milk and no sugar, please.

W Is fat-free milk okay?

M _____

(a) Okay, I'll take a little sugar.

(b) Thanks, would you like a cup?

(c) This is the best coffee in town.

(d) I prefer whole milk, if you have it.

20

M Does this car get good mileage?

W For a sports car, the mileage is excellent.

M Good. I like to save money on gas.

W _____

(a) Sure, I'd love to go for a ride.

(b) Then this is the model for you.

(c) It's less than a mile down the road.

(d) We have a bunch of vehicles for sale.

21

W I hope you can come to my son's school play tonight.

M I'm planning on it!

W Wonderful. I can drive us both, if you'd like.

M _____

(a) I love going to the theater.

(b) My son does well in school, too.

(c) Sorry, I won't be able to make it.

(d) Carpooling sounds like a great idea.

22

M My last final is tomorrow. I've really got to study.

W I'm so happy I already finished all of mine.

M How do you think you did?

W _____

(a) At 8 in the morning.

(b) It was to be a really hard test.

(c) The library's great for studying.

(d) Not great, but not terrible either.

23

W Do you have any plans for the weekend?

M My wife and I are going camping at a national park.

W What fun! Do you camp often?

M _____

(a) It's too cold to be outside.

(b) Almost every chance we get.

(c) Thanks, have a great weekend.

(d) Sure. I'll start setting up the tent.

24

M How do you feel about your dorm room?

W It's a little small, but it gets plenty of sunlight.

M You're lucky. Mine doesn't even have a window!

W _____

(a) No, I prefer the window open.

(b) Actually, I'm not feeling very well.

(c) I can't believe how sunny it is today.

(d) Yeah, but you have a lot more space.

25

W I'm thinking about quitting.

M What if you can't find another job?

W It shouldn't be hard. I have lots of experience.

M _____

(a) What kind of benefits do you offer?

(b) I don't think you should ask for a raise.

(c) Even so, the job market is slow these days.

(d) I'm interested in applying for the open position.

26

M What seems to be the problem?

W I sent my document to the printer, but it hasn't printed yet.

M Did you check the machine for jams?

W _____

(a) It's due this afternoon.

(b) It's a brand-new printer.

(c) Yes, that's not the problem.

(d) I need to print a larger copy.

27

W I need my travel visa as soon as possible.

M It usually takes about two weeks.

W How can I speed up the process?

M _____

(a) I hope you enjoy your trip.

(b) I'll need to inspect your visa.

(c) You can pay extra for express service.

(d) You should carry your passport at all times.

28

M Hi, Jan. What've you been doing lately?

W I'm really busy at work right now.

M Oh? Lots of overtime?

W _____

(a) I'll be there as soon as I can.

(b) Yeah, almost two hours a day.

(c) I'm sorry, I'm going home early today.

(d) Yeah, everything at work is calmer.

29

W Want to pop out for a sandwich?

M The deli's probably closed already.

W Really? What time is it?

M _____

(a) Turkey and cheese.

(b) Just around the corner.

(c) I know. I'm so hungry.

(d) I'm not sure, but it's late.

30

W Hello. I have an appointment to see Dr. White.

M You must be Ms. Sullivan. Here are some forms for you to fill out.

W Okay. Will the doctor be able to see me soon?

M _____

(a) Do you have an appointment?

(b) Your health insurance has expired.

(c) The pleasure's all mine, Ms. Sullivan.

(d) He'll be ready for you in five minutes.

31

W Hi, can I help you?

M Who do I speak to about opening a new account?

W I can do that for you. What kind of account are you interested in?

M Savings.

W Okay. Here's a brochure that describes our different savings accounts.

M Thanks. I'll look this over and get back to you.

Q: What is the man mainly doing?

(a) Reviewing a copy of a brochure.

(b) Getting information on bank accounts.

(c) Checking his savings account balance.

(d) Helping the woman open a new account.

32

W Do you accept reservations in advance?

M Yes, we do.

W Great. I'd like to make one for this Friday at 8 o'clock.

M How many people will be dining in your party?

W There will be ten of us in total.

Q: What are they mainly discussing?

(a) Daily menu options.

(b) Invitations to a dinner.

(c) The schedule of a party.

(d) A restaurant reservation.

33

M Wow, what a game last night! Did you see it?

W No. I don't follow soccer very closely.

M Our team scored at the end to win the game.

W That's great. Does that mean they're playing in the finals this weekend?

M Right. The game's at 3:30 on Saturday.

W I'll try to catch this one.

Q: What is mainly being discussed?

(a) Ordering tickets to a sporting event.

(b) A schedule change for a soccer game.

(c) The accomplishment of a sports team.

(d) The speakers' plans for the upcoming weekend.

34

W Have you bought all your supplies yet?

M No. I still need a couple of books and another notebook.

W You'd better hurry. Classes start in two days!

M I know. I'm going shopping tomorrow.

W Oh, can I come with you? I need to buy some pens.

M Sure. We can go tomorrow morning.

Q: What are they mainly discussing?

(a) Going out to dinner.

(b) Shopping for groceries.

(c) Registering for classes.

(d) Getting school materials.

35

M Did you go to the new store yesterday?

W Yeah, but I wasn't impressed.

M Really? Why not?

W They didn't have a good selection of science fiction titles.

M You should put in a request with customer service.

W I did. They're ordering more.

Q: What is mainly being discussed?

(a) What the man likes to read.

(b) The woman's new job at a store.

(c) Different science fiction novels.

(d) The woman's opinion of a bookstore.

36

W Kevin, do you have a minute?

M Sure. What's going on?

W I need someone to look over this article I wrote. It's due tomorrow.

M No problem. I'll be happy to.

W Thanks so much. Just email me your comments when you're finished.

M At your work address?

W Yeah, that'd be best.

Q: What is mainly taking place?

(a) The woman is asking the man for a favor.

(b) The man is helping the woman find an address.

(c) The man is giving an assignment to the woman.

(d) The woman is sharing some information with the man.

37

W Are you okay, Simon?

M I'm worried about Megan.

W Your friend from work? Is she alright?

M She's scheduled to have surgery today.

W Oh, I didn't know. Don't worry, I'm sure she'll be fine.

M I know. But I can't stop thinking about it.

Q: What is the main topic of the conversation?

(a) The woman's upcoming surgery.

(b) The man's concern for his coworker.

(c) A problem with their work schedule.

(d) A health problem the man is having.

38

M How's the apartment hunt going?

W Well, I've pretty much stopped looking.

M Why? I thought you hated your current place.

W It's not the best, but every other option is too expensive.

M So you've decided not to move?

W I'm afraid I don't have much choice.

Q: Which is correct about the woman?

(a) She wants the man to help her move.

(b) She is starting to look for a new home.

(c) She is not going to change her apartment.

(d) Her current apartment is too expensive.

39

W Sean, a word about your term paper?

M Sure, Professor. Was there a problem with it?

W Not at all. I loved it!

M Oh, that's a relief.

W In fact, you should submit it to the National Essay Contest.

M How do I go about doing that?

W I'll pass you all the info by email.

Q: Which is correct about the man?

(a) He won a contest.

(b) He wrote a school paper.

(c) He got a new email address.

(d) He signed up for the woman's class.

40

M Have you made any summer vacation plans yet?

W I want to travel to Europe, but I haven't bought tickets yet.

M Why not?

W I need to find someone to go with me. I don't want to go alone.

M I have a friend who might be interested.

W Really? That'd be great!

M I'll give her your number.

Q: Which is correct according to the conversation?

(a) The woman already knows the man's friend.

(b) The woman doesn't like traveling by herself.

(c) The woman's friends canceled their travel plans.

(d) Both the man and the woman are going to Europe.

41

W I just signed up to run the charity marathon next month.

M I've been meaning to do that.

W You should. The money they raise goes toward a good cause.

M Yeah. But I've never run in such a long race.

W Neither have I. Just remember, it's not a competition.

M You're right. The important thing is raising money for the charity. I'll do it.

Q: Which is correct according to the conversation?

(a) Both speakers frequently run in races.

(b) The woman organized the charity run.

(c) The man will participate in the marathon.

(d) The man works for a charity organization.

42

W Has Dave rented a car for the trip yet?

M Yes, and he got a great deal. Only 25 dollars a day.

W How did he do that?

M I think he knows someone at the rental agency.

W That's incredible. With the money we're saving, we can take a longer trip.

M Uh-huh. Remember to thank Dave next time you see him.

Q: Which is correct about Dave?

(a) He is a good driver.

(b) He is currently on vacation.

(c) He owns a car rental business.

(d) He received a discount on a car.

43

M I suddenly feel like I have to sneeze.

W Do you have a cold?

M No, it seems more like an allergy.

W Oh, I hope it's not my cat.

M A cat? I'm afraid that's probably what's causing the reaction.

W In that case, let's go sit on the patio instead.

M Okay, I appreciate it.

Q: What can be inferred about the man?

(a) He is allergic to cats.

(b) He needs to see a doctor.

(c) He is suffering from a cold.

(d) He thinks it's too cold on the patio.

44

M You shouldn't eat so many fried foods, Beth.

W I've tried to cut back, but it's hard to find healthy meals at restaurants.

M Why don't you cook at home more?

W Well, I'm not a very good cook.

M Let me lend you a cookbook. It focuses on healthy recipes that are simple and delicious.

W That sounds nice. I guess I could try cooking.

Q: What can be inferred from the conversation?

(a) The woman wants to open a restaurant.

(b) The woman will invite the man to dinner.

(c) The man thinks he eats too many fried foods.

(d) The man thinks cooking at home is better for health.

45

W Good evening, sir. How may I help you?

M I'm in town for a business conference, and I need a room for three nights.

W Very good. We're having a special promotion right now—stay three nights and get the fourth night free.

M Hmm... that sounds nice, but I'm afraid I'm needed back at the office the day after the conference ends.

W I see, of course. I'll have someone show you to your room immediately.

M Thank you.

Q: What can be inferred about the man?

(a) He will choose to extend his stay.

(b) He will be at the hotel for three nights.

(c) He will receive a discounted room rate.

(d) He will give a presentation at the conference.

46

Automobiles were available in the U.S. in the early 1900s, but they were rather expensive. Henry Ford helped to improve the situation. In 1913, he introduced the first production assembly lines in the factories of his Ford Motor Company. The assembly line method made it possible to produce more cars at a lower cost and with less labor. Prices for automobiles dropped more than half, and before long the car had become an important part of American culture and enterprise.

Q: What is mainly being discussed?

(a) The life story of businessman Henry Ford.

(b) The invention of the automobile in America.

(c) American car culture in the nineteenth century.

(d) The effect of assembly lines on reducing the price of American cars.

47

Mr. Howard, this is Diana Smith calling from Dr. Sims' office. According to our calendar, you have an appointment for a general checkup this Thursday afternoon at 2:30. Dr. Sims was wondering whether it would be okay with you to push this back to Friday. Any time during the morning or afternoon would be fine. Please give me a call to let me know if this will work for you. Thanks.

Q: What is Ms. Smith's purpose for calling Mr. Howard?

(a) To recommend a doctor.

(b) To reschedule an appointment.

(c) To inform him of some test results.

(d) To ask why he missed his appointment.

48

If you toss and turn in bed all night, then RestBetter is for you. This unique new product has been called by doctors the most effective way to treat insomnia. Its special blend of vitamins and sedatives ensures that you'll get a good night's sleep. But best of all, you don't have to worry about side effects.

Q: What is being introduced?
(a) An insomnia treatment.
(b) An addiction clinic.
(c) A medical procedure.
(d) A custom-made mattress.

49

Skin cancer is often considered less serious than cancer of the internal organs, but it can be just as deadly. One common cause of skin cancer is frequent exposure to the sun. The sun gives off radiation that can damage the skin and ultimately lead to a cancerous growth. The best way to prevent this damage is by covering skin with clothing when outside. Sunscreen should be applied to any skin not covered by clothing.

Q: What is the main topic of the talk?
(a) How sunscreen works.
(b) How to treat a bad sunburn.
(c) How to prevent skin cancer.
(d) How skin cancer was discovered.

50

Good afternoon, sales employees. I have a special announcement for you. This afternoon, you will all have the opportunity to give blood to the local blood bank. A blood donation van will be in the parking lot from 1:30 to 5 o'clock. Anyone who wishes to give blood may do so during these hours. Thank you.

Q: What will some employees do this afternoon?
(a) Go to the hospital.
(b) Donate their blood.
(c) Attend a sales meeting.
(d) Deliver a gift to charity.

51

New York City has always had problems with crime. There is good news, however. Over the last decade and a half, violent crime rates have consistently decreased. 2007 was the first year since 1963 that the number of murders was below 500. Moreover, New York now has the lowest crime rate of any of the ten largest cities in the United States. While there's still room for improvement, most residents are pleased with the progress.

Q: What is the main idea of the talk?
(a) New York City is safer than it once was.
(b) Police are failing to stop crime in New York.
(c) Residents approve of New York's government.
(d) There are too many murders in large American cities.

52

The XPhone 2.0 is much more than a cellular phone. With 50 gigabytes of memory space, it's practically a home computer. Many different kinds of software are available for the XPhone. You can install your favorite music players, watch movies, play video games, and surf the net. It also has a camera function, which is much more advanced than those of other camera phones.

Q: What is mainly being advertised?
(a) How to add memory to your phone.
(b) The features of a multi-purpose mobile.
(c) The products sold at an electronics store.
(d) Different software packages for cell phones.

53

There's a new trend in the pet industry: snakes. All over the country, pet stores are reporting record sales of snakes and snake-related products. Unfortunately, people don't know how to care for a pet snake. Many of the animals die after only a short time, and others escape from their owners and enter the wild. In response to this, states are considering controlling who is able to buy pet snakes and how many they are able to own.

Q: Which is correct about owners of pet snakes?
(a) Their numbers have decreased in recent years.
(b) They usually capture their snakes from the wild.
(c) Some of them are unprepared to care for the animals.
(d) Laws prohibit them from owning more than one snake.

54

Generally, we view television as a hindrance to a child's education. But that may just depend on what they're watching. A long-term study looked at children who were shown televised nature documentaries on a regular basis and analyzed their later educational development. On average, children who developed a habit of viewing nature shows later scored higher on college placement exams than a random sampling from the general population.

Q: Which is correct about nature documentaries?
(a) They are not frequently televised.
(b) They are shown in college classrooms.
(c) They can improve educational performance.
(d) They encourage people to protect the environment.

55

There are many types of pollution. The one that receives the least amount of attention is pollution caused by light. In urban areas, the collective glare from thousands of city lights can be very strong. The effect is harmful to animals that rely on darkness to hunt or need the light of the stars and moon for navigation. Light pollution can even harm people. Studies show extreme light pollution causes headaches, fatigue, and stress.

Q: Which is correct about light pollution?
(a) It is a problem in the countryside.
(b) It can cause depression in people.
(c) It is the most harmful kind of pollution.
(d) It disrupts animals' sense of direction.

56

When bones weaken, there is an increased risk that they can fracture or break, leading to serious health problems. A disease called osteoporosis affects bones in this way. For some reason, osteoporosis is most common in older women, but it can also attack men and younger people. Medical experts recommend that people of all ages drink milk, which contains calcium. Calcium helps bones develop and grow, so a diet high in calcium may prevent osteoporosis.

Q: Which is correct about calcium?
(a) Most older women lack it.
(b) It can help keep bones strong.
(c) It is used to cure osteoporosis.
(d) Bones cannot grow without it.

57

Sound effects are an important part of any film. The person responsible for creating these effects is known as the foley artist. The sounds are recorded separately, in a sound studio, and added to the film later. Foley artists often use common, everyday objects to create their sound effects. For example, to imitate the sounds of a fist fight, a foley artist might crack a piece of bamboo or strike a watermelon. These artificial sounds make the movie scene more dramatic.

Q: Which is correct about foley artists?
(a) They do their work in a recording studio.
(b) They help actors produce dramatic sounds.
(c) Their job is to create sounds for car chase scenes.
(d) They sometimes work with visual special effects artists.

58

The genre of the Western, in both literature and film, is where we frequently meet "the drifter" archetype. The drifter mysteriously appears in town one day. No one knows who he is or where he came from. Against his will, he gets pulled into a local dispute, most often at the behest of a new female friend. Due to his superior skills with a pistol, he manages to defeat the villain and save the townsfolk. Typically, the story closes with the drifter riding off, still mysteriously, into the sunset.

Q: What can be inferred about "the drifter?"
(a) He solves problems through violence.
(b) Western films sometimes end with his death.
(c) He retains the same name in different stories.
(d) The archetype has no basis in historical fact.

59

Many scientists have tried to prove the existence of extrasensory perception, or ESP. ESP is the ability to obtain information about something without using the five senses. Because of this, it is often referred to as a "sixth sense." In some studies, subjects have been able to successfully identify objects without looking at or feeling them. This suggests that they may indeed possess a type of extrasensory perception. However, no experiment has been found that can consistently demonstrate the existence of ESP.

Q: What can be inferred about ESP?
(a) It has been disproved.
(b) Some people have it, but others do not.
(c) There is no scientific consensus about it.
(d) Researchers are no longer interested in it.

60

James Joyce is considered by many scholars to be one of the greatest authors. His 1922 novel *Ulysses* is certainly a masterpiece. But despite his talent, Joyce didn't receive much popular recognition during his lifetime. He and his wife and children were constantly in financial trouble. He also had a number of health issues, including failing eyesight. Though originally from Dublin, Ireland, Joyce spent most of his adult life in other cities in Europe. He died at the age of 58 in Zurich, Switzerland.

Q: What can be inferred from the lecture?
(a) Joyce published many novels.
(b) Joyce's wife was from Switzerland.
(c) Joyce became more famous after his death.
(d) The book *Ulysses* was a financial success.

Actual Test 2

1

M That concert was a lot of fun, wasn't it?

W _____

(a) Yeah, the guitar lessons are going well.

(b) Actually, I'm not the biggest jazz fan.

(c) Tickets go on sale next Friday.

(d) Okay, see you there!

2

W Who designed your interior? I love it!

M _____

(a) Thanks. The couch goes over there.

(b) It was a local firm—JDS Associates.

(c) Sure. Let me introduce you to my friend.

(d) I prefer spending my free time outdoors.

3

M I feel awful about infecting your computer with a virus.

W _____

(a) If you aren't feeling well, go to the hospital.

(b) I hope you can prevent it from happening.

(c) Right, the new anti-virus software.

(d) No harm done. It's been removed.

4

W What's your take on the Rogers deal?

M _____

(a) I believe it's still on sale.

(b) Okay. I'll call a meeting about it.

(c) I'd rather not judge it prematurely.

(d) Rogers? I don't think I've met him.

5

M Did you hear? They're giving us tomorrow off.

W _____

(a) I'm afraid I'll have to come in anyway.

(b) Between seven and ten vacation days.

(c) I'll see you at the office, in that case.

(d) Let me check my schedule.

6

W This restaurant is completely understaffed.

M _____

(a) I know. We've been waiting for ages!

(b) Would you mind leaving the tip?

(c) I'll have the special of the day.

(d) No, I'd rather go for Chinese.

7

M I just burned myself on the stove!

W _____

(a) Here, put this ice pack on it.

(b) Use the front burner instead.

(c) Yes, the oven and stove are electric.

(d) Don't worry. Dinner will be ready soon.

8

W Is this the number for the tourist information office?

M _____

(a) Just give them a call.

(b) No. That one's outdated.

(c) It's my first time visiting, too.

(d) Yes, here's a brochure on the area.

9

M I'm sorry, what did you say your name was?

W _____

(a) No, I didn't catch her name, either.
(b) It's Maria, but you can call me Mary.
(c) Don't apologize. It's a common mistake.
(d) Please allow me to introduce Ms. Kathy Arnold.

10

M I forgot my wallet. Could you lend me a couple of bucks?

W _____

(a) The price has been heavily discounted.
(b) I'm afraid I can't spare a dime.
(c) Better check with the police.
(d) It's a high-interest loan.

11

W Who was it that called just now?

M _____

(a) Shall I take a message?
(b) I never saw one before.
(c) A guy trying to sell something.
(d) You can put my name down.

12

W Hey, David just told me the news. Congratulations!

M _____

(a) I'm really glad it was.
(b) I know. Let's plan a surprise party for him.
(c) Thanks. I've been after this promotion for months.
(d) That's very kind. I'd appreciate any help you can give.

13

M How is it you got here so fast during rush hour?

W _____

(a) Not for another hour or so.
(b) Traffic was a nightmare.
(c) I'd avoid the freeway.
(d) I took the subway.

14

W It must be difficult moving around on crutches like that.

M _____

(a) The insurance covers everything.
(b) The doctor diagnosed the disease.
(c) If you want, I can push your wheelchair.
(d) Yeah, but you get used to it after a while.

15

M Did Janet mention that the appointment's been pushed back?

W _____

(a) Let me consult the agenda and get back to you.
(b) Uh-huh. She's really looking forward to it.
(c) She did. To 5:30 instead of 5, right?
(d) Yes, I'll straighten it right away.

16

M Tell me again where the convenience store is?
W At 5th and Longview, by the gas station.
M What's the exact address?
W _____

(a) I'm not sure, but you can't miss it.
(b) Go ahead and fill it up.
(c) Somewhere on the other side of town.
(d) A gallon of milk and a dozen eggs, please.

17

W What would you like from the cafeteria, tea or coffee?
M I'm going to stick with water for now, thanks.
W Are you sure I can't get you anything?
M _____

(a) Sure, I'd love to join you.
(b) Two sugars and some cream.
(c) The cafeteria's on the ground floor.
(d) Maybe a couple of napkins if you can.

18

M Hi, Linda. Did you see the basketball game last night?

W Sorry, Jim. I can't talk right now.

M I guess you're pretty busy today.

W _____

(a) Let me know if I can give you a hand.

(b) No, I wasn't able to play.

(c) Yeah, the project's due this afternoon.

(d) Thanks for asking. It was really entertaining.

19

W Give Meagan a call at her house.

M I just did. No one answered.

W That's odd. Where do you think she is?

M _____

(a) We'll meet her there.

(b) I haven't the faintest idea.

(c) She just called from work.

(d) I'm going to the laundromat.

20

M I got a letter from the Pearson Graduate School today.

W Well... what did it say?

M They're giving me a full scholarship.

W _____

(a) Costs for grad school can be high.

(b) So, are you going to apply for it?

(c) Pearson isn't the best school.

(d) Wow, I'm so proud of you.

21

W Can you direct me to the nearest ATM?

M The hotel lobby has one. It's by the vending machines.

W Does it accept all major cards?

M _____

(a) Enter your PIN.

(b) There's a bank around the corner.

(c) Not sure. I've never used it.

(d) You can check in whenever you'd like.

22

W Where are you traveling today, sir?

M My final destination is Mumbai, but I'm stopping in Dubai for a night.

W Which would you prefer, a window or aisle seat?

M _____

(a) Something close to the front of the plane, please.

(b) I don't know. I haven't been before.

(c) Here, you can have my seat.

(d) Yes, that's where I'm from originally.

23

M Your mother's been in the hospital for a while. How's she doing?

W Oh, she's hanging in there for now.

M If there's anything I can do for you, just let me know.

W _____

(a) That's okay. I have to visit her every day.

(b) Thanks so much. I'll keep the offer in mind.

(c) You could make an appointment, if you'd like.

(d) The doctor says the medicine will take effect soon.

24

M I've been trying to access this site all day, but it refuses to load.

W The tech guys are on it. They say the server's down.

M When do they think they'll have it up and running again?

W _____

(a) Try turning your computer on.

(b) The site's been shut down.

(c) Should be any time now.

(d) I'll call for tech support.

25

W Do you know when your calculus class meets?

M According to my schedule, it's Mondays and Wednesdays from 11 to 1:30.

W Hey, I think that's the same class I'm in.

M _____

(a) Let me check out my schedule.
(b) Not really. Professor Kim is quite strict.
(c) I've never been too good at math myself.
(d) Great. It'll be nice having someone to sit with.

26

M I'm thinking of having a barbecue up at my lake house next weekend.

W Oh, that sounds like a really good time. Who are you inviting?

M Just a handful of good friends. Would you like to come?

W _____

(a) I'll help you put together an invite list.
(b) Sorry, I can't throw parties at my house.
(c) Where's the barbecue going to take place?
(d) Definitely. Do you want me to bring anything?

27

W Someone told me there's a drive-in theater in this neighborhood.

M There is. It's on Coleridge Avenue, about three or four miles past the park.

W I'm not too familiar with that area. I thought it had a problem with crime.

M _____

(a) The shows start around 8 pm every evening.
(b) Sure, let's go tomorrow night and check it out.
(c) It's unsafe late at night, but the movies end early.
(d) I know what you mean. Drive-ins aren't popular anymore.

28

M I'm supposed to give a World War II history presentation in class next month.

W You should talk to Harry Mills. I'm sure he could tell you some interesting stories.

M Hmm... who's that?

W _____

(a) I can't think of his name just now.
(b) A local author who served in the war.
(c) Yes, I'd be happy to help you prepare.
(d) Your professor sounds like a smart man.

29

W Are there any houses for rent in your neighborhood?

M Yes, but they're all very expensive.

W That's okay. I'm willing to pay up to a thousand a month.

M _____

(a) The area is quiet and very safe.
(b) Sorry, that's much too expensive.
(c) I'll send you a rental contract to sign.
(d) In that case, I might have one for you.

30

M What seems to be the problem with your vehicle?

W The ignition is acting up. Sometimes I go to start it and nothing happens.

M I see. I'll check things out and let you know the verdict later today.

W _____

(a) I need to return my rental.
(b) Great, thanks for the ride.
(c) The sooner, the better.
(d) Okay, I'll take it!

31

M My name is Sam Park. I have a reservation.

W Okay, Mr. Park. It looks like you've reserved three nights in a single room.

M That's correct.

W May I see your credit card and photo ID, please?

M Here you are. And I'll need assistance taking my bags to my room.

Q: What is the man mainly doing?
(a) Checking into a hotel.
(b) Applying for a photo ID.
(c) Booking his accommodations.
(d) Asking for help with his luggage.

32

W Michael, you look stressed.

M I'm not surprised. Things have been crazy at work lately.

W You should take better care of yourself.

M What do you suggest?

W They say taking a short nap every day reduces stress.

M That's interesting. Maybe I'll try it.

Q: What is the main topic of the conversation?

(a) The man's well-being.

(b) How to recognize stress.

(c) The man's work schedule.

(d) How to increase productivity.

33

M Do you have any pets, Susan?

W Yes, a dog and two cats.

M My wife wants to get a dog, but I'm not sure it's a good idea.

W Why's that?

M I don't know if we'll have time to take care of it.

W I'm sure you can make time if that's really what she wants.

Q: What is mainly being discussed?

(a) The woman's three pets.

(b) How to take care of a dog.

(c) How to increase one's free time.

(d) The man's wife's desire for a dog.

34

W I see I'll be responsible for gas and electricity.

M Yes, all our tenants pay for those.

W Do you know how much?

M Not more than fifty dollars a month.

W That seems quite low. Are you sure?

M Pretty sure. You can check with our current tenants if you'd like.

W Okay, please send me their contact information.

Q: What is being discussed?

(a) The rent charged for an apartment.

(b) A building's renovation costs.

(c) The utility costs on a rental property.

(d) Tenant satisfaction levels.

35

M Hello. I'd like to sign up for the volleyball league.

W Do you have any experience with the sport?

M No, not really.

W We'll put you in the beginner's division, then. Here's the sign-up form.

M Great. How much is it?

W The fee is thirty dollars, and that's good for a whole year.

Q: What is the man doing?

(a) Renewing his gym membership.

(b) Practicing his volleyball skills.

(c) Meeting his volleyball team.

(d) Registering for a volleyball club.

36

W Carl, a friend and I are going up to visit the historical park this weekend.

M I've always wanted to do that.

W You're welcome to come along.

M Really? How are you getting there?

W By train. The commuter line stops right across the street.

M Okay. I think I might join you.

Q: What is the woman doing?

(a) Giving information about a train schedule.

(b) Describing a tourist attraction to the man.

(c) Reporting on last weekend's trip.

(d) Inviting the man on an outing.

37

M Wheeler's new model is billed as the best mountain bike on the market.

W Yeah... I'm not convinced.

M Why not?

W It's basically the same as their model from last year, which underperformed.

M Are you saying it's all hype?

W I think they just repackaged a mediocre product.

M You could be right.

Q: What is the main topic of the conversation?

(a) A company's marketing ploy.

(b) The man's new mountain bike.

(c) The woman's views on a sport.

(d) An unsuccessful product launch.

38

W Hello. I need to make a doctor's appointment.

M What seems to be the problem?

W I think I twisted my ankle playing basketball yesterday.

M Does it hurt when you stand on it?

W Yes. I'm having a lot of trouble walking.

M Okay. Let me see if the doctor is available today.

Q: Which is correct about the woman?

(a) She needs her ankle seen to.

(b) She was playing basketball today.

(c) She missed her doctor's appointment.

(d) She is worried about her health insurance.

39

M The news from the office isn't good.

W Do you mean the layoffs?

M They'll be announced tomorrow.

W Don't worry. I'm sure your job is safe.

M There's no guarantee. It's not like I'm irreplaceable.

W Come on. I think you're selling yourself short.

Q: Which is correct about the man?

(a) He must select workers to lay off.

(b) He thinks the woman will be fired.

(c) He is upset about the woman's news.

(d) He doubts his job is safe.

40

W Tell me how the painting looks, Jack. Is it hanging straight?

M Tilt it a little to the right.

W Great. What do you think?

M To be honest, I feel it would look better on the opposite wall.

W Oh? What makes you say that?

M The color of this wall is too light. The painting looks out of place on it.

Q: Which is correct about the man?

(a) He thinks the painting should be moved.

(b) He thinks the wall needs to be repainted.

(c) He thinks the painting is unattractive.

(d) He thinks the painting is still crooked.

41

M Have you been over to the new Vietnamese restaurant, Sally?

W Yes, I was there just yesterday for lunch. It was delicious.

M You think so? I wasn't too impressed. My beef was overcooked and too salty.

W I had the tofu soup, and the flavors were wonderful.

M Maybe I should give that a try.

W I'm going again tomorrow if you'd like to come.

Q: Which is correct according to the conversation?

(a) The woman is anxious to order the beef.

(b) The woman thought her dish was too salty.

(c) The man enjoyed his meal at the restaurant.

(d) The man is willing to try the restaurant again.

42

W What's the name of our business class text?

M *Small Business in the Modern World.*

W I take it you've already purchased it, then?

M That's right. It was pretty expensive—around a hundred dollars.

W That's awful. I've already spent hundreds on my other books.

M If you want, you can share mine until you get your own.

W Thank you, but I might as well buy it now.

Q: Which is correct according to the conversation?

(a) The woman will buy her own book.

(b) The man has already taken the class.

(c) The woman cannot afford a textbook.

(d) The business class does not require a text.

43

M Joanna, I've got two tickets to the horserace tomorrow. Care to join me?

W Oh, I love the races! But I have to go into the office tomorrow.

M Well, it doesn't start till 4:30.

W Hmm... I'm supposed to stay until 5.

M Can't you ask your boss to let you go a little early?

W I will, but don't get your hopes up.

Q: What can be inferred about the woman?
(a) She's upset with her boss.
(b) She doesn't care for sports.
(c) She doesn't think she can attend.
(d) She wants to work late tomorrow.

44

W Good morning. I need to move some money around between my accounts.

M Okay, and what types of accounts do you have with us?

W Checking and savings. I'd like to transfer everything from the savings and close it out.

M Just so you know, we do charge a 25-dollar closing fee for that.

W Even if I'm putting the money into my checking account?

M Yes, it's bank policy.

W Well, I need to do this, so I guess I'll pay it.

Q: What can be inferred about the woman?
(a) She will keep both accounts open.
(b) She is hoping to open a new account.
(c) She was unaware of the bank's policy.
(d) She is uncertain about how to proceed.

45

M What can you tell me about this computer monitor?

W Its picture quality is very high.

M Is that why it's so expensive? This other one is bigger but much cheaper.

W That's right. Size doesn't always mean better quality.

M Well, for me, I need the image to be as sharp as possible.

W I'd recommend the first one, in that case.

Q: What can be inferred from the conversation?
(a) Both monitors are being offered at discounted prices.
(b) The woman thinks the smaller model is a bad deal.
(c) The man feels the smaller monitor is costly.
(d) The man will purchase the larger model.

46

The island of Socotra, though technically a part of Yemeni territory, is vastly different from the mainland in terms of flora. Its peculiarities are a result of its relative isolation in the Indian Ocean; it lies 350 kilometers south of the Arabian Peninsula. Over the millennia plants native to the island evolved undisturbed by outside influences. The result is a wide array of species that are found nowhere else on Earth, such as Socotra's emblematic dragon's blood tree.

Q: What is mainly being discussed?
(a) An island's unique plant life.
(b) The evolution of a tree species.
(c) The location of a Yemeni island.
(d) Exploration of Indian Ocean islands.

47

Proponents of a technique known as art therapy believe that human creativity can accomplish more than producing beautiful works of art. Specifically, they feel the process of creating art can be used to treat certain emotional, cognitive, and even physical disorders. Art therapists guide their patients through carefully designed creative tasks, with the aim of helping them come to terms with trauma, fear, and repressed emotions. Though widely practiced, art therapy has yet to receive endorsements from official mental health governing bodies.

Q: What is mainly being introduced?
(a) Characteristics of art produced by mental patients.
(b) An artistic form of mental health treatment.
(c) The similarities between artists and therapists.
(d) The ability of art to express difficult subjects.

48

Your attention. This is Kaitlin Wong, and she's coming onboard as head of Human Resources. Kaitlin has many years of experience in the industry, and she's offered some exciting ideas for revamping the department. If you have any questions for her, I encourage you to stop by her office this afternoon. Let's all give her a warm welcome.

Q: What is the speaker mainly doing?
(a) Asking for feedback from employees.
(b) Introducing a new department manager.
(c) Announcing some changes to the department.
(d) Congratulating a supervisor on her promotion.

49

One of the richest men in American history started out as an immigrant child of modest means. Andrew Carnegie, born in Scotland, arrived in Pennsylvania with his parents in 1848. He took on various low-paying jobs at an early age, but his natural business acumen enabled him to rapidly rise through the ranks at a state railroad company. Before long, he had accumulated enough wealth to make widespread investments, and in the 1870s he founded the Carnegie Steel Company.

Q: What is the main topic of the talk?
(a) Background on Carnegie's success in business.
(b) Immigrants' contributions to America.
(c) Carnegie's railroad innovations.
(d) Carnegie's family history.

50

Today's consumer keeps an average of 25 electronic gadgets in the home. That number was just three back in 1980. One outcome of this surge in electronic products is increased demand for household electricity. But high power consumption is bad for the environment, so many are advocating stricter efficiency standards for all electronic goods.

Q: What is the main topic of the talk?
(a) Possible methods for lowering electricity use.
(b) The effect of power consumption on the planet.
(c) A negative consequence of electronics' popularity.
(d) Efforts to discourage the use of electronics products.

51

Don't let tax season get you down. This year, put your own personal tax advisor to work with SymaTech's Tax Works Pro. Have complicated investments? Work and live abroad? Own rental property? None of these issues are problems for Tax Works Pro, which contains automatically updated databases on every facet of tax law.

Q: What is mainly being discussed?
(a) Financial software.
(b) Investment advice.
(c) A tax advisory firm.
(d) Changes to tax policy.

52

Traditional language education, as practiced in government-run schools around the world, involves textbook lessons and intra-class conversation practice. Is it any wonder that so many students fail to achieve fluency in a foreign language? To truly tackle another tongue, it is necessary to live in it, 24-7. Study abroad programs offer students this opportunity. Immersed in a foreign culture, they have no choice but to learn to speak as those around them do. You'd be amazed at the results this can produce.

Q: What is the main idea of the talk?
(a) Language education must balance linguistic and cultural learning.
(b) Schools should discontinue their traditional language classes.
(c) Studying abroad is the best way to learn a language.
(d) Textbooks have no place in language study.

53

Excuse me, please. This is an announcement for passengers on Blue Sky Airlines flight 5-5-1 to London. At this time, we would like to ask anyone flying with small children, or anyone requiring extra assistance, to please board the plane. You may do so at the gate marked B-6. Once everyone in this first group of passengers is aboard, we'll continue boarding starting with our first-class passengers. Thank you.

Q: Who should board the plane now?
(a) Passengers sitting in the rear of the plane.
(b) Customers with first-class tickets.
(c) All passengers flying to London.
(d) Parents with young children.

54

One percent of people around the world suffer from rheumatoid arthritis or RA, a debilitating disorder of the body's joints. The main element of RA is an inflammation of the components that make up our joints, which can lead to bone and cartilage damage. Moreover, the pain this causes can significantly reduce a person's mobility. Traditional treatment involves painkillers and physical therapy, though a number of pharmacological remedies are currently under development.

Q: Which is correct about rheumatoid arthritis?
(a) There is a certain amount of pain associated with it.
(b) It is affecting a growing segment of the population.
(c) Conventional remedies have not been effective.
(d) It attacks cells found in the interior of the bones.

55

After over 80 years of service to the community, the Springdale Public Library is in danger of shutting its doors. In recent years, borrower numbers have plummeted, and state-mandated funding has all but dried up. If the library is to be saved, we must demonstrate its continued relevance. Please, stop by, browse its catalogues, sign up for a membership card, and leave with an armful of quality reading. You won't regret it.

Q: Which is correct about the library?
(a) It plans to downsize its staff.
(b) It is being shut down by the state.
(c) It requires a membership card to borrow books.
(d) It is announcing a special offer for new members.

56

In the early 1800s, scientists from several nations were working on a way to transmit messages quickly over long distances. The result was the electrical telegraph, a technology capable of sending a signal from one telegraph station to another via previously laid electrical cables. The first practical telegraph system was established in the United States between Baltimore and Washington, D.C. in 1844. 1861 saw the creation of the first transcontinental line, and in 1866 a cable was successfully laid between the U.S. and Europe.

Q: Which is correct according to the talk?
(a) Telegraph lines were capable of crossing oceans.
(b) The electrical telegraph was invented in Baltimore.
(c) Electrical telegraph technology existed before 1800.
(d) An American inventor created the concept of telegraphy.

57

Ever since wireless Internet technology was introduced, restaurants, bars, and coffee shops have made use of it to attract business. In return for a small purchase, customers can enjoy unlimited access to the web at no charge. But the current economic hardships are causing some to reconsider this policy. Establishments in cities worldwide are becoming concerned with the costs of the electricity consumed by customer laptops and of maintaining a network. Increasingly, wi-fi seekers are finding it more difficult to locate access points where they feel welcome.

Q: Which is correct according to the report?
(a) Most restaurants will soon ban the use of laptops.
(b) Wireless access is more prevalent in larger cities.
(c) Wireless network costs have recently increased.
(d) Offers of free wi-fi access are being rethought.

58

The fifth annual Stratton Folk Music Festival will begin next weekend and last for ten days. This year, we've booked more bands than ever before, and they'll be playing folk styles from all over the world. Also, for the first time, there will be food vendors on site so you can enjoy delicious local treats while you listen to the music. Tickets can be purchased at City Hall, and remember: as always, children get in free.

Q: What can be inferred about the music festival?
(a) There are special children's activities.
(b) It has been held only once before.
(c) It has expanded since last year.
(d) There is no charge to enter.

59

There are various contenders for the first "modern novel," but Cervantes' *Don Quixote* is generally credited as such. In it, Cervantes utilized the conventions of medieval storytelling, which featured the adventures of heroic characters related in short, disjointed tales. However, though episodic, the stories found in *Don Quixote* are much more cohesive, furthering a single plot. This is what earns the work recognition as a modern novel.

Q: What can be inferred about modern novels?
(a) They use medieval stories as templates.
(b) They do not include more than one plot.
(c) They differ widely from Cervantes' work.
(d) They tend to be less episodic and more cohesive.

60

For years, childcare experts have promoted children's participation in sports to build teamwork skills, increase socialization, and keep physically fit. Recently, however, these promotions have slowed. Numerous studies now suggest that children do not benefit from the competitive aspect of sports activities. In fact, some experts feel that it can be harmful. Instead, they recommend engaging children in cooperative pursuits, such as community projects and art and music clubs. While childhood sports are certainly not expected to disappear, they may become less popular as time goes on.

Q: What can be inferred from the talk?
(a) The benefits of sports may not outweigh the drawbacks.
(b) Physical fitness is not as important as it once was.
(c) It is recommended that children not play sports.
(d) Art and music clubs are viewed as competitive.

Actual Test 3

1

W Excuse me, do you have the time?

M _____

(a) Yes, it will be soon.
(b) Sorry, time for what?
(c) Yes, it's ten after nine.
(d) I don't have any free time right now.

2

M I have a really bad headache.

W _____

(a) Are you all right now?
(b) I have some pills here.
(c) Don't worry. Headaches aren't painful.
(d) I took something for it.

3

W How long does it take to get to Anyang?

M _____

(a) I go every day.
(b) I go by subway.
(c) Usually it's only 10 minutes.
(d) It's between Seoul and Suwon.

4

W I've been promoted to senior manager.

M _____

(a) When will that happen?
(b) Thank you for saying so.
(c) This calls for a celebration!
(d) Please give him my congratulations.

5

M Did anyone call while I was at lunch?

W _____

(a) You missed a phone call.
(b) I can't come to the phone right now.
(c) I'm afraid you have the wrong number.
(d) Your wife tried to reach you.

6

M I really need someone to sub for me tomorrow.

W _____

(a) Please, be my guest.
(b) May I ask you a favor?
(c) I'm sorry. I need it right now.
(d) I'm available. I have the day off.

7

W Hi, Jake! How's it going?

M _____

(a) Not too bad, thanks.
(b) No, I was just leaving.
(c) I'd better be on my way.
(d) It'd be a pleasure to meet him.

8

W Could you give me a wakeup call, please?

M _____

(a) No problem. What time?
(b) Sure. I'll call back in a few minutes.
(c) Of course. Where can we reach you?
(d) Certainly, we'll send someone to your room.

9

M Chill out! Why are you so uptight?

W _____

(a) I'm sorry to let you down.
(b) I'm really nervous about flying.
(c) I love to take it easy on the weekends.
(d) My muscles are sore from too much exercise.

10

W I hate it when sales clerks chat on their cell phones instead of serving their customers.

M _____

(a) Do you really mean it?
(b) Yeah, they do seem to be very busy.
(c) I wish they'd bring a menu over.
(d) They don't seem to take any pride in their work.

11

M I work twelve-hour days all week.

W _____

(a) I thought you were more ambitious.
(b) Why don't you look for another job?
(c) I didn't realize you were job-hunting.
(d) How long have you been out of work?

12

W Which is your teacher?

M _____

(a) She's pretty good, really.
(b) The one with long blonde hair.
(c) She teaches English literature.
(d) A class of twenty-five students.

13

M I'd never felt so humiliated in my life!

W _____

(a) I'm disappointed in you.
(b) Don't bother me just now.
(c) I'm having a really bad day.
(d) You must have felt really small.

14

M I love the new decor in your living room.

W _____

(a) Our architect was fantastic.
(b) The lounge looks good, too.
(c) A landscaper did the design.
(d) An interior designer did it.

15

M Who are you going to the dance with—Sam or Justin?

W _____

(a) I think they'll both be there.
(b) Neither. I'm going with Paul.
(c) Slow dances are his favorite.
(d) I don't think Sam likes Justin.

16

W Do you want to go to the Summer Jazz concert tonight?
M Sure, I've got nothing going on this evening.
W When shall we meet?
M _____

(a) How about 7:30?
(b) Call me after midnight.
(c) What about in the main lobby?
(d) Let's make it by the front gate.

17

M Do you think I'm eligible for the new tax cuts?
W I'm not sure. Why don't you call the Tax Department?
M I called several times, but I couldn't get through.
W _____

(a) Don't go there, just call them.
(b) Yeah, their line is always busy.
(c) Their phone number is right here.
(d) They're pretty easy to get a hold of.

18

W Excuse me. Do you have a minute?
M I guess so. What do you need?
W Could you tell me where the nearest ATM is?
M _____

(a) Let's have a look around.
(b) I'm sorry, I'm a tourist, too.
(c) I don't know the instructions.
(d) There's a mailbox on the corner.

19

W Make yourself at home. Can I get you a drink?

M A coffee would be lovely, thanks.

W How do you like your coffee?

M _____

(a) I don't like it at all.

(b) I'll have a cappuccino to go.

(c) Black with two sugars, please.

(d) I like drinking coffee after meals.

20

W I love French perfume.

M Let me buy you some for your birthday.

W Thank you... How does this one smell on me?

M _____

(a) Mmm. It's divine!

(b) Let me see how you look.

(c) I'll put it on my credit card.

(d) This is the best moisturizer ever!

21

W You look really nervous.

M Our English class is doing a play for the whole school tonight.

W Your English is good. You'll be fine.

M _____

(a) I'll do it tomorrow instead.

(b) I need to stay at home tonight.

(c) You're right. I'd better not go.

(d) But I've never been in a play before.

22

M How can I get to your house tonight, Jenny?

W Exit the expressway at Cedar Heights.

M Okay. And then what?

W _____

(a) Go past the mall, and take the second right.

(b) The real-estate office is just past the school.

(c) You'll find the community center on your left.

(d) Then head over to where we are.

23

M At last! I've finished for the week.

W Yeah, I'm off too.

M Have a good weekend!

W _____

(a) See you tomorrow!

(b) I'll be back on Friday.

(c) Thanks. See you next week.

(d) I'm always happy on the weekends.

24

W This is my new dorm room.

M Well... it's somewhat small.

W Don't you like it?

M _____

(a) I had another room.

(b) It's a bit too spacious.

(c) Let me see your other rooms.

(d) I'd need more space than this.

25

W I really want to improve my English by studying overseas.

M You're too young to live in a foreign country.

W What if I study in Korea next year and do an exchange the year after?

M _____

(a) I think you should study abroad.

(b) Sure. Stay in Korea another semester.

(c) Why don't you do your exchange here?

(d) Yes, in another year you'll be old enough.

26

W Hi, darling! What are you doing?

M I'm chatting online with my friends.

W What does LOL stand for?

M _____

(a) Nothing really.

(b) Don't worry. You'll get it.

(c) It means "laugh out loud."

(d) You'll get the hang of it soon.

27

M Excuse me. Is this the French Embassy?

W Yes, it is. What can I do for you?

M How do I get a tourist visa for France?

W _____

(a) How much money do you have?

(b) That depends on if it's in France.

(c) You have to leave France first, then apply for a visa.

(d) Korean citizens can stay for 3 months without a visa.

28

W Hi, Frederick! How are things?

M Great, thanks. How's your new job?

W It's OK, but I hate working nights. It's so antisocial.

M _____

(a) You need some friends who are day workers.

(b) Why don't you like being around other people?

(c) Try to enjoy yourself when you go out in the evenings.

(d) True. You have to work when everyone else is going out.

29

W What's the matter?

M I've had enough of apartment hunting.

W Didn't you like the last apartment we looked at?

M _____

(a) Exactly.

(b) Probably.

(c) Surely not.

(d) Not really.

30

M Is this the plastic surgery department?

W Yes, it is. How can I help you?

M I'd like to make an appointment for Friday morning.

W _____

(a) Do you need to cancel?

(b) We don't do consultations.

(c) Why don't you have surgery today?

(d) I'm sorry, the doctor is all booked up that day.

31

W I've lost my ATM card, and I'm calling to ask when the replacement will arrive.

M It usually takes ten working days.

W Can you tell me how much is left in my account?

M You've got $101.00.

W That's good. Thank you.

Q: What is the woman doing in the conversation?

(a) Withdrawing money.

(b) Applying for a new card.

(c) Opening a bank account.

(d) Checking her account balance.

32

W We need to reserve a restaurant for my mother's 60th.

M Yeah. Where would she like to go?

W Not Thai or Mexican; she can't eat spicy food.

M How about the new Chinese place?

W The food there is too bland.

M Well then, let's go French.

W The sauces will be too heavy.

Q: What is the woman's main concern?

(a) Making a dinner reservation.

(b) Choosing the best recipe to cook.

(c) Selecting a foreign food restaurant.

(d) Finding a restaurant her mother will like.

33

M England crushed Belgium seven to nothing last night.

W How many games have they won now?

M Seven in a row.

W So they have a perfect qualifying record?

M Yep. Belgium didn't seriously attempt a goal.

W Sounds like England dominated the match.

Q: What is mainly being discussed?

(a) The result of the initial playoffs.

(b) England's position in the playoff.

(c) Belgium's score in the soccer game.

(d) The defeat of Belgium at soccer game.

34

M Can you order me a copy of *Sociology* Today?

W Certainly. It'll be about two weeks.

M Two weeks! All university syllabuses have to be submitted by Monday.

W Could you explain that again?

M I need that book to write my syllabus.

W I'll see what I can do.

Q: What is the man's main concern?

(a) He wants to do a new course.

(b) He can't write without the book.

(c) The bookstore is uncooperative.

(d) He needs the textbook to plan his course.

35

W I don't agree with this at all!

M What's the article about?

W It's about mothers who move overseas with their children who're studying abroad.

M I think it's a matter of cultural attitudes.

W It's not right! Mothers should focus on their own lives and let their kids live theirs.

M I guess I see your point.

Q: What is being discussed?

(a) How to secure a study abroad opportunity.

(b) How culture influences family relationships.

(c) How much mothers should be with their children.

(d) How beneficial it is for children to study abroad.

36

M Shall we sit here by the window?

W Sure. Do you mind if I smoke?

M I don't think you can do that in here.

W Really? Well, where can I go?

M We could sit in the courtyard.

W Yeah, but it's beginning to rain.

Q: What is the woman's problem?

(a) She doesn't like sitting outside.

(b) She wants to sit with her friend.

(c) There are no free tables.

(d) She can't smoke anywhere.

37

M You're looking pretty strained these days. What's wrong?

W My mother is behaving quite strangely.

M What do you mean?

W Well, sometimes she doesn't seem to know where she is.

M That's pretty worrying. What are you going to do?

W I want her to have some tests, but it'll be a struggle getting her to go.

Q: What is the woman mainly worried about?

(a) Finding where her mother is.

(b) Her mother's confused state.

(c) The stress in her mother's life.

(d) Her mother's attitude towards doctors.

38

W What did you think of the apartments we saw today?

M The first one was interesting.

W I can't pinpoint what was wrong, but I didn't like that one.

M It was in a cul-de-sac, which isn't so safe at night.

W How about the second one?

M Nice, but overpriced.

W I guess we'll have to keep looking.

Q: What does the man think about the apartments?

(a) Seeing them in the dark was difficult.

(b) He's not sure why he doesn't like them.

(c) One has bad access; the other is undervalued.

(d) Neither are suitable to live in.

39

W Doctor, I've been having problems with my ankle.

M Well, ankles are very prone to injury and pain.

W What do you think is causing it?

M I can't say offhand. It's a very complex joint.

W Can you run some tests?

M Yes, that's what we'll do.

Q: Which is correct about the man?

(a) He doesn't think he can treat the ankle.

(b) He can't do tests on intricate joints like ankles.

(c) He doesn't believe the woman's ankle is hurting.

(d) He cannot predict the cause of the pain.

40

M Here's a website offering a free e-Book about Italian holidays!

W What does it cost?

M It looks like it's free.

W There's got to be a catch.

M This guy just wants to share his favorite places in Italy.

W Yeah, and I bet his sister works in the Italian travel industry.

M Actually, you're right! How did you know?

Q: Which is correct about the couple?
(a) The man is very cynical.
(b) The woman doesn't want to go to Italy.
(c) The man is more naive than the woman.
(d) The woman has seen the advertisement before.

41

M I think I'll apply for the New York City Marathon this year.

W You must be crazy! Last year three older men died in the marathon.

M I'll start training now, then.

W It takes months to train. Do you know how long a marathon is?

M About 26 kilometers, I think.

W No, it's 26 miles!

Q: Which is correct about the man?
(a) He thinks the race is longer than it is.
(b) He is very optimistic about his fitness.
(c) He hasn't run a marathon for a few years.
(d) He is still young enough to be competitive.

42

M Let's buy a rental property while house prices are low.

W Are bank-owned homes still coming onto the market?

M Yes, there are about 5,000 current foreclosures in this area.

W So how strong is the demand for rental homes now?

M There is a housing excess. We may have to offer a lower rent.

W Still, in the long term it's a good investment.

Q: Which is correct according to the conversation?
(a) Many renters are investing in real estate.
(b) There is a big demand for homes to rent.
(c) Most rental properties are owned by the banks.
(d) There may not be enough tenants to fill a rental property.

43

W Do you prefer cats or dogs as pets?

M Well, they each have their good points.

W I agree. But I like the fact that cats are more independent.

M Sometimes too independent.

W Maybe, but you don't have to bathe them or clip their nails.

M True, but I enjoy going for walks with a dog.

W Cats take care of their own exercise needs.

Q: What can be inferred from the conversation?
(a) The man doesn't like cats.
(b) The man likes independent pets.
(c) The woman hasn't had a pet dog.
(d) The woman prefers low-maintenance pets.

44

W If you're going out, put some sunscreen on.

M I'll only be gone thirty minutes.

W In this weather you can burn in ten minutes.

M It's too late to worry about that.

W What do you mean?

M Skin cancer is caused by our sun exposure as children.

W Children spend a lot more time in the sun, but what we do as adults is important too.

Q: What can be inferred from the conversation?
(a) The woman thinks the sun is dangerous for children.
(b) The man thinks he won't get sunburned on his walk.
(c) The woman doesn't think children need to worry about the sun.
(d) The man doesn't think adult actions can influence skin cancer risk.

45

W Professor, I couldn't enroll in your class.

M This semester I'm only teaching English majors.

W But I really want to have you as a teacher again.

M I'm sorry, you'll need to enroll through your major.

W But your class times suit my schedule.

M There's nothing I can do about it.

W I don't think this is fair.

Q: What can be inferred from the conversation?
(a) The woman is not majoring in English.
(b) Students were not informed about the changes.
(c) This is the first time enrollment has been restricted.
(d) The woman is aware of the new university policies.

46

Lev Vygotsky was a Russian psychologist who died in Moscow in 1934 at the age of 38. After his death, some of his work was sent to London, where it was recognized as groundbreaking thought in developmental psychology. However, it wasn't until the 1960s that Vygotsky's ideas were published in English, and they did not reach a wide audience until a compilation of his work was published in 1978. Since then many of his concepts, including the "zone of proximal development" (ZPD) and "scaffolding" have become key ideas in early childhood education.

Q: What is the main idea of the passage?
(a) Vygotsky did not write in English.
(b) Developmental psychology began in the late 1930s.
(c) Psychology has contributed a lot to early childhood education.
(d) Vygotsky's ideas took a long time to affect educational theory.

47

This is Veronica Shaw calling. I may have to be back at work by the 22nd of July rather than the 27th. Can you tell me whether it's possible to change my plane ticket, and if so, how much extra would it cost? If you're able to call me back at this number tomorrow that would be great. Thanks.

Q: Why did the woman call?
(a) To check about upgrading her flight.
(b) To ask the adjusted cost of her plane ticket.
(c) To find out if changing her ticket is a possibility.
(d) To tell her travel agent her holiday dates might change.

48

Today's speaker, Malcolm Brown, is the author of three best-selling English grammar books. Mr. Brown started out as an English teacher, just like yourselves. However, the worksheets he wrote for his students were so popular, and explained English grammar so simply and clearly, that he was approached by a publisher and retired from teaching. For the past twenty years, Malcolm has been working on different language editions of his famous grammar books. Today he'll talk about *Teaching Grammar in a Changing World*. Give Malcolm Brown a big hand.

Q: What is the purpose of the introduction?
(a) To explain why the speaker gave up teaching.
(b) To sell the speaker's publications to the audience.
(c) To give background information about the speaker.
(d) To improve the speaker's reputation among teachers.

49

Blue-collar jobs are known to have associated health risks, but there is mounting evidence that white-collar workers are adversely affected by hours spent working on computers. Research studies from Japan and India suggest that workers in many occupations, including teaching, are experiencing health problems such as glaucoma and eThrombosis, besides a host of other minor complaints.

Q: What is the main idea of the talk?
(a) Most workers experience health problems.
(b) Teachers use computers too much in their work.
(c) Manual labor is no more dangerous than an office job.
(d) Professionals are experiencing work-related health hazards.

50

Good morning, staff. As you know, our Human Resources Department wants to survey all of you to determine current employee satisfaction levels at the company. Please take a few minutes to complete this short questionnaire. To ensure anonymity, do not include your name or other identifying remarks, and seal your completed survey in the envelope provided. No individuals will be quoted: all answers will be summarized and included in a group report.

Q: What is the main point of the announcement?
(a) To thank workers for filling out a survey.
(b) To reassure workers about survey confidentiality.
(c) To explain the workplace's employment policy.
(d) To convince employees that they are treated fairly.

51

Juvenile delinquency is commonly regarded as a comparatively recent problem, but it has been recognized as a crime in the U.S. since the early 1800s, when statistics on delinquency began to be recorded. In fact, delinquency levels in 1820 were higher than in 2009, when figures were quite low. Juvenile delinquency peaked in the late 1950s, at which time it was also realized that delinquency knows no class distinctions.

Q: What is the main argument of the talk?
(a) Youth crime is not a serious problem today.
(b) More young people committed crimes in the 1950s.
(c) Criminal activity among the young is not a new phenomenon.
(d) Crime among young people was most prevalent in the 1820s.

52

The Harvard Liberal Arts Faculty has decided to publish academic articles online, in order to freely share "its academic wealth." The decision, part of the growing open-access movement in academic circles, is seen as a major blow to scholarly journals. Critics of the move cite the crucial importance of the peer-review process in academic scholarship. However, reducing the power of scholarly journals to make or break academics' careers by acceptance or rejection of research papers is also seen by many as an important consequence of the decision.

Q: What is the talk mainly about?
(a) How academic articles are published.
(b) The disadvantages of academic journals.
(c) The impact of Harvard's online article initiative.
(d) The impact of peer-review on professors' careers.

53

The Army Corps of Engineers reports that costs have risen on an essential part of New Orleans' flood protection system. Since work began last year, the estimated cost of three flood gates and a storm surge barrier has risen to $1.8 billion. The structures are essential to the plan to close off the Inner Harbor Navigation Canal. Army Corps officials have asked Congress for another $540 million so that work can be completed by 2011. Congress originally allocated $14.3 billion to build an improved flood protection system for New Orleans.

Q: Which is correct according to the report?
(a) The cost of the project has risen by $1.8 billion.
(b) Costs of the New Orleans project are rising steeply.
(c) Lack of funds has caused slow progress in the project.
(d) The flood protection system is taking longer than anticipated.

54

Today's lecture is about James Cook, an English farm boy who rose to command his own ship during one of the British Empire's first great scientific expeditions. Patrons helped him join the merchant navy, which he later left for the Royal Navy. His genius for precision in navigation changed the way the world was mapped and allowed Britain to gain control of North America. Cook was then given command of the scientific expedition to the Pacific Ocean, to observe the transit of Venus from Tahiti, and to search for the legendary Southern Continent.

Q: Which is correct according to the lecture?
(a) Cook is remembered for his rags-to-riches story.
(b) The merchant navy was not interested in creating maps.
(c) Cook had an outstanding talent for cartographic accuracy.
(d) The Southern Continent was discovered by British explorers.

55

The Green IT Report, released today, shows that green policies have finally become important to IT companies. Most of the companies surveyed are considering green policies, and spending on sustainable technology is rising. In fact, the report reveals that IT companies are starting to lead the way in corporate green initiatives. The high price that the IT industry pays for energy is stimulating their search for energy-efficient products.

Q: Which is correct according to the news release?
(a) IT companies have pioneered new energy sources.
(b) IT products are easily adapted to green technology.
(c) The IT industry is changing its outlook on the environment.
(d) The computer industry doesn't care about the environment.

56

After a decade of sensational growth, Starbucks is facing stiff competition and an economic climate that makes people reassess their spending on luxury items. Starbucks chief executive, Howard Schultz, is seeking to recapture the magic of the early Starbucks years, when customers were excited by the quality of the coffee and the neighborhood coffeehouse feel of its stores. New refurbishments seek to increase the "theater" of the Starbucks experience, with baristas more visible and local stores featuring individual themes.

Q: Which is correct according to the talk?
(a) Starbucks has never lost its unique ambience.
(b) Starbucks branches will be made less uniform.
(c) The quality of Starbucks coffee has decreased recently.
(d) Many people regard Starbucks coffee as a necessity of life.

57

Jane Austen is one of the most widely read and loved English writers. Her reputation rests on four novels published during her lifetime, and two more released posthumously. This small literary output is matched by the dearth of autobiographical material about Austen. Only a few of her estimated 3,000 letters remain, the majority having been burned or censored by her sister Cassandra. Her work received little favorable review during her lifetime, and until the late 1800s she was appreciated only by the literary elite.

Q: Which is correct about Jane Austen according to the talk?
(a) Contemporary writers recognized her genius.
(b) Her sister destroyed early drafts of her work.
(c) Most of her novels were published after her death.
(d) She has been regarded as a great writer for 100 years.

58

Tired of the same old vacations? Ready for excitement and challenge? Then join Extreme Sports New Zealand for the vacation of a lifetime. Travel with a small group of other thrill seekers and experience New Zealand's rugged unspoiled environment as you challenge your personal limits daily. Travel the South Island's mountains, rivers, and coasts for two weeks of water-touch bungee jumping, swimming with dolphins, sea kayaking, ice climbing, glacier walks, skydiving, and, most exciting of all, whitewater rafting.

Q: What can be inferred from the advertisement?
(a) Only a few people will be allowed to join this trip.
(b) The tourism company places a high priority on safety.
(c) No special skills are required to participate in the activities.
(d) People of any age are welcomed by Extreme Sports New Zealand.

59

Professor Robert Solomon of the University of Texas at Austin teaches a 24-lecture course on the emotions. Solomon believes understanding emotions is a key to understanding the meaning of life. Many of his conclusions run counter to common sense. He argues that emotions are intelligent and rational, and are essential to survival. In these lectures, you will witness a contemporary philosopher assessing, rejecting, accepting, or refining the ideas of the greatest philosophical thinkers of the past.

Q: What can be inferred from the advertisement?
(a) Solomon's philosophy has little to say about feelings.
(b) The lectures are unlikely to be intellectually stimulating.
(c) Solomon believes that emotions have rational basis.
(d) Western philosophical tradition has always emphasized the emotions.

60

Scientists are concerned that the depleted ozone layer over the Southern Ocean is fueling strong winds that prevent the ocean from soaking up the greenhouse gas carbon dioxide. Simultaneously, these strong winds are dredging up deep-water carbon dioxide, causing acidification of the ocean. Scientists worry that these changes in pH levels could damage organisms at the bottom of the food chain, such as plankton, krill, and fish larvae.

Q: What can be inferred from the report?
(a) The ozone hole is larger than was previously thought.
(b) The problems are not affecting the Northern Hemisphere.
(c) Ozone depletion might endanger entire marine ecosystems.
(d) Strong winds are directly affecting the ocean's largest organisms.

Actual Test 1

Answer Keys

🎧 Listening Comprehension

1	(d)	7	(d)	13	(b)	19	(d)	25	(c)	31	(b)	37	(b)	43	(a)	49	(c)	55	(d)
2	(b)	8	(c)	14	(b)	20	(b)	26	(c)	32	(d)	38	(c)	44	(d)	50	(b)	56	(b)
3	(a)	9	(c)	15	(b)	21	(d)	27	(c)	33	(c)	39	(b)	45	(b)	51	(a)	57	(a)
4	(d)	10	(b)	16	(c)	22	(d)	28	(b)	34	(d)	40	(b)	46	(d)	52	(b)	58	(a)
5	(b)	11	(b)	17	(b)	23	(b)	29	(d)	35	(d)	41	(c)	47	(b)	53	(c)	59	(c)
6	(b)	12	(c)	18	(d)	24	(d)	30	(d)	36	(a)	42	(d)	48	(a)	54	(c)	60	(c)

📝 Grammar

1	(a)	6	(a)	11	(a)	16	(d)	21	(d)	26	(b)	31	(c)	36	(c)	41	(b)	46	(a)
2	(b)	7	(d)	12	(b)	17	(d)	22	(a)	27	(d)	32	(d)	37	(b)	42	(b)	47	(c)
3	(c)	8	(a)	13	(a)	18	(a)	23	(b)	28	(d)	33	(d)	38	(d)	43	(d)	48	(d)
4	(a)	9	(b)	14	(d)	19	(b)	24	(b)	29	(d)	34	(d)	39	(d)	44	(d)	49	(d)
5	(d)	10	(b)	15	(a)	20	(c)	25	(d)	30	(a)	35	(a)	40	(d)	45	(c)	50	(a)

🔊 Vocabulary

1	(a)	6	(a)	11	(a)	16	(c)	21	(a)	26	(c)	31	(b)	36	(a)	41	(c)	46	(c)
2	(b)	7	(b)	12	(d)	17	(a)	22	(b)	27	(a)	32	(a)	37	(d)	42	(d)	47	(b)
3	(c)	8	(d)	13	(a)	18	(b)	23	(a)	28	(a)	33	(d)	38	(d)	43	(b)	48	(a)
4	(a)	9	(c)	14	(b)	19	(d)	24	(d)	29	(a)	34	(a)	39	(a)	44	(d)	49	(c)
5	(a)	10	(a)	15	(c)	20	(a)	25	(c)	30	(d)	35	(a)	40	(c)	45	(a)	50	(d)

✎ Reading Comprehension

1	(b)	5	(c)	9	(d)	13	(c)	17	(a)	21	(b)	25	(d)	29	(a)	33	(d)	37	(b)
2	(c)	6	(a)	10	(c)	14	(c)	18	(b)	22	(c)	26	(b)	30	(a)	34	(a)	38	(a)
3	(c)	7	(b)	11	(b)	15	(b)	19	(d)	23	(c)	27	(d)	31	(c)	35	(a)	39	(c)
4	(d)	8	(a)	12	(d)	16	(b)	20	(a)	24	(a)	28	(c)	32	(a)	36	(c)	40	(d)

Actual Test 2

Answer Keys

🎧 Listening Comprehension

1	(b)	7	(a)	13	(d)	19	(b)	25	(d)	31	(a)	37	(a)	43	(c)	49	(a)	55	(c)
2	(b)	8	(b)	14	(d)	20	(d)	26	(d)	32	(a)	38	(a)	44	(c)	50	(c)	56	(a)
3	(d)	9	(b)	15	(c)	21	(c)	27	(c)	33	(d)	39	(d)	45	(c)	51	(a)	57	(d)
4	(c)	10	(b)	16	(a)	22	(a)	28	(b)	34	(c)	40	(a)	46	(a)	52	(c)	58	(c)
5	(a)	11	(c)	17	(d)	23	(b)	29	(d)	35	(d)	41	(d)	47	(b)	53	(d)	59	(d)
6	(a)	12	(c)	18	(c)	24	(c)	30	(c)	36	(d)	42	(a)	48	(b)	54	(a)	60	(a)

✏️ Grammar

1	(d)	6	(b)	11	(c)	16	(a)	21	(c)	26	(a)	31	(b)	36	(a)	41	(c)	46	(b)
2	(b)	7	(c)	12	(b)	17	(d)	22	(a)	27	(a)	32	(b)	37	(c)	42	(d)	47	(d)
3	(b)	8	(b)	13	(a)	18	(a)	23	(c)	28	(c)	33	(a)	38	(b)	43	(b)	48	(a)
4	(a)	9	(b)	14	(b)	19	(b)	24	(c)	29	(c)	34	(a)	39	(a)	44	(b)	49	(c)
5	(b)	10	(d)	15	(b)	20	(d)	25	(c)	30	(d)	35	(b)	40	(d)	45	(c)	50	(d)

📢 Vocabulary

1	(a)	6	(b)	11	(b)	16	(c)	21	(b)	26	(b)	31	(c)	36	(c)	41	(a)	46	(c)
2	(c)	7	(a)	12	(a)	17	(a)	22	(a)	27	(a)	32	(c)	37	(d)	42	(b)	47	(b)
3	(c)	8	(b)	13	(d)	18	(b)	23	(b)	28	(a)	33	(b)	38	(a)	43	(a)	48	(a)
4	(b)	9	(a)	14	(d)	19	(b)	24	(a)	29	(d)	34	(a)	39	(b)	44	(d)	49	(d)
5	(c)	10	(a)	15	(b)	20	(c)	25	(d)	30	(c)	35	(a)	40	(b)	45	(d)	50	(b)

✒️ Reading Comprehension

1	(a)	5	(a)	9	(c)	13	(d)	17	(b)	21	(d)	25	(c)	29	(c)	33	(c)	37	(a)
2	(c)	6	(a)	10	(d)	14	(b)	18	(b)	22	(c)	26	(b)	30	(b)	34	(b)	38	(c)
3	(b)	7	(b)	11	(c)	15	(b)	19	(c)	23	(a)	27	(d)	31	(d)	35	(d)	39	(c)
4	(d)	8	(a)	12	(a)	16	(a)	20	(a)	24	(b)	28	(c)	32	(c)	36	(a)	40	(a)

Actual Test 3

Answer Keys

🎧 Listening Comprehension

1	(c)	7	(a)	13	(d)	19	(c)	25	(d)	31	(d)	37	(b)	43	(d)	49	(d)	55	(c)
2	(b)	8	(a)	14	(d)	20	(a)	26	(c)	32	(d)	38	(d)	44	(d)	50	(b)	56	(b)
3	(c)	9	(b)	15	(b)	21	(d)	27	(d)	33	(d)	39	(d)	45	(a)	51	(c)	57	(a)
4	(c)	10	(d)	16	(a)	22	(a)	28	(d)	34	(d)	40	(c)	46	(d)	52	(c)	58	(a)
5	(d)	11	(b)	17	(b)	23	(c)	29	(d)	35	(c)	41	(b)	47	(c)	53	(b)	59	(c)
6	(d)	12	(b)	18	(b)	24	(d)	30	(d)	36	(d)	42	(d)	48	(c)	54	(c)	60	(c)

📝 Grammar

1	(a)	6	(b)	11	(a)	16	(a)	21	(d)	26	(d)	31	(b)	36	(a)	41	(a)	46	(d)
2	(d)	7	(d)	12	(c)	17	(b)	22	(a)	27	(c)	32	(d)	37	(d)	42	(b)	47	(a)
3	(a)	8	(c)	13	(d)	18	(b)	23	(c)	28	(a)	33	(b)	38	(b)	43	(d)	48	(b)
4	(b)	9	(b)	14	(c)	19	(a)	24	(a)	29	(a)	34	(b)	39	(d)	44	(c)	49	(c)
5	(b)	10	(d)	15	(d)	20	(d)	25	(d)	30	(d)	35	(b)	40	(c)	45	(d)	50	(a)

📣 Vocabulary

1	(c)	6	(a)	11	(a)	16	(a)	21	(a)	26	(c)	31	(a)	36	(c)	41	(d)	46	(d)
2	(d)	7	(b)	12	(d)	17	(d)	22	(d)	27	(b)	32	(d)	37	(b)	42	(a)	47	(a)
3	(a)	8	(c)	13	(b)	18	(d)	23	(b)	28	(a)	33	(b)	38	(c)	43	(b)	48	(a)
4	(b)	9	(d)	14	(b)	19	(c)	24	(c)	29	(d)	34	(c)	39	(d)	44	(d)	49	(c)
5	(d)	10	(a)	15	(a)	20	(a)	25	(a)	30	(d)	35	(a)	40	(a)	45	(c)	50	(b)

✒️ Reading Comprehension

1	(a)	5	(c)	9	(d)	13	(c)	17	(a)	21	(b)	25	(d)	29	(c)	33	(b)	37	(d)
2	(d)	6	(c)	10	(a)	14	(b)	18	(a)	22	(b)	26	(d)	30	(c)	34	(b)	38	(d)
3	(b)	7	(b)	11	(d)	15	(b)	19	(c)	23	(a)	27	(c)	31	(d)	35	(b)	39	(c)
4	(d)	8	(c)	12	(d)	16	(c)	20	(c)	24	(d)	28	(b)	32	(c)	36	(d)	40	(d)

 TEPS 등급표

등급	점수	영역	능력검정기준(Description)
1+급 Level 1+	901~990	전반	**외국인으로서 최상급 수준의 의사소통 능력** 교양 있는 원어민에 버금가는 정도로 의사소통이 가능하고 전문분야 업무에 대처할 수 있음. (Native Level of Communicative Competence)
1급 Level 1	801~900	전반	**외국인으로서 거의 최상급 수준의 의사소통 능력** 단기간 집중 교육을 받으면 대부분의 의사소통이 가능하고 전문분야 업무에 별 무리 없이 대처할 수 있음. (Near-Native Level of Communicative Competence)
2+급 Level 2+	701~800	전반	**외국인으로서 상급 수준의 의사소통 능력** 단기간 집중 교육을 받으면 일반분야 업무를 큰 어려움 없이 수행할 수 있음. (Advanced Level of Communicative Competence)
2급 Level 2	601~700	전반	**외국인으로서 중상급 수준의 의사소통 능력** 중장기간 집중 교육을 받으면 일반분야 업무를 큰 어려움 없이 수행할 수 있음. (High Intermediate Level of Communicative Competence)
3+급 Level 3+	501~600	전반	**외국인으로서 중급 수준의 의사소통 능력** 중장기간 집중 교육을 받으면 한정된 분야의 업무를 큰 어려움 없이 수행할 수 있음. (Mid Intermediate Level of Communicative Competence)
3급 Level 3	401~500	전반	**외국인으로서 중하급 수준의 의사소통 능력** 중장기간 집중 교육을 받으면 한정된 분야의 업무를 다소 미흡하지만 큰 지장 없이 수행할 수 있음. (Low Intermediate Level of Communicative Competence)
4+급 Level 4	201~400	전반	**외국인으로서 하급 수준의 의사소통 능력** 장기간의 집중 교육을 받으면 한정된 분야의 업무를 대체로 어렵게 수행할 수 있음. (Novice Level of Communicative Competence)
5+급 Level 5	10~200	전반	**외국인으로서 최하급 수준의 의사소통 능력** 단편적인 지식만을 갖추고 있어 의사소통이 거의 불가능함. (Near-Zero Level of Communicative Competence)

i-TEPS Review

국내 최초 통합 영어능력 평가
*in*tegrated-TEPS

⇨ **의사소통에 필요한 듣기, 말하기, 읽기, 쓰기 능력을 통합하여 평가한다.**
듣기, 말하기, 읽기, 쓰기 능력은 서로 밀접한 관계를 가진 요소로 듣기, 읽기 능력 혹은 말하기, 쓰기 능력만을 단순히 측정해서는 정확한 영어능력을 평가하기 어렵다. *i*-TEPS는 유기적인 연관성을 지닌 이 네 가지 의사소통 능력을 통합적으로 측정하여 수험자의 영어능력을 정확하게 평가한다.

⇨ **변별력과 신뢰도가 있는 시험이다.**
i-TEPS는 국내 최고 권위의 영어능력 평가로 듣기, 읽기 분야에서 탁월한 변별력을 인정받은 TEPS와 국내 최초 CBT 방식의 영어 말하기·쓰기 시험인 TEPS-Speaking & Writing의 성공 노하우를 바탕으로 개발되었다. 실전 영어능력을 보다 정밀하게 측정할 수 있도록 세분화된 채점 요소를 적용하고 있으며, 출제자와 채점자를 어학 분야의 최고 전문가들로 선정하여 높은 신뢰도와 탁월한 변별력을 지니고 있다.

⇨ **실전 영어능력을 측정한다.**
간단한 대화를 할 수 있는 능력부터 도표를 보고 발표하는 분석력과 구성력까지, 접하는 상황에 따라 필요한 영어능력도 다양하다. *i*-TEPS는 유학이나 비즈니스 등 특정한 분야에서의 영어 활용 능력을 집중적으로 평가하는 타 시험과는 달리, 비즈니스 상황을 포함한 다양한 영어 사용 환경을 재현하여 실질적으로 활용 가능한 영어능력을 평가한다.

⇨ **경제성과 효율성을 갖춘 시험이다.**
i-TEPS는 타 통합 영어능력 평가시험에 비해 응시료가 저렴하다. 한 번의 시험으로 듣기, 말하기, 읽기, 쓰기 능력을 종합적으로 평가하여 각각의 영역을 별도로 평가해야 하는 타 시험과 비교해도 응시료 부담이 적다. *i*-TEPS는 최소의 시간과 비용으로 수험자의 영어능력을 정확히 측정하는 높은 효율성을 갖춘 시험이다.

i-TEPS 영역별 유형 및 설명

i-TEPS는 기존의 TEPS와 TEPS-Speaking & Writing 시험을 토대로 듣기, 말하기, 읽기, 쓰기 능력을 종합적으로 측정하는 통합형 시험으로 개발되었다. Listening, Grammar & Vocabulary, Reading, Speaking, Writing의 5개 영역에 걸쳐 약 3시간 동안 진행되며, 총 143문항, 400점 만점으로 구성되어 있다.

영역		문제유형	문항수	시간		총점
Listening	Part 1	짧은 대화를 듣고 이어질 대화로 가장 적절한 답 고르기	15	35분		80점
	Part 2	긴 대화를 듣고 질문에 가장 적절한 답 고르기	15			
	Part 3	담화를 듣고 질문에 가장 적절한 답 고르기	10			
Grammar & Vocabulary	Part 1	대화문의 빈칸에 가장 적절한 답 고르기	15	20분		20점
	Part 2	단문의 빈칸에 가장 적절한 답 고르기	15			
	Part 3	대화문의 빈칸에 가장 적절한 어휘 고르기	15			20점
	Part 4	단문의 빈칸에 가장 적절한 어휘 고르기	15			
Reading	Part 1	지문을 읽고 빈칸에 가장 적절한 답 고르기	10	40분		80점
	Part 2	지문을 읽고 질문에 가장 적절한 답 고르기 (1지문 1문항)	19			
	Part 3	지문을 읽고 질문에 가장 적절한 답 고르기 (1지문 2문항)	6			
Speaking	Part 1	간단한 질문에 대답하기	1(3)		답변 10초	100점
	Part 2	소리내어 읽기	1	준비 30초	답변 45초	
	Part 3	일상 대화 상황에서 질문에 답하기	1(5)	준비 15초	답변 10초	
	Part 4	그림 보고 연결하여 이야기하기	1	준비 60초	답변 60초	
	Part 5	도표 보고 발표하기	1	준비 120초	답변 90초	
Writing	Part 1	받아쓰기	1	10분		100점
	Part 2	이메일 쓰기	1	15분		
	Part 3	의견 쓰기	1	30분		
계						400점

TEPS

Test of English Proficiency
developed by
Seoul National University

TEPS

Test of English Proficiency
developed by
Seoul National University

성명 Name	한글 영문	

수험번호
Registration No.

문제지번호
Test Booklet No.

감독관확인란

청해
Listening Comprehension

문법
Grammar

어휘
Vocabulary

독해
Reading Comprehension

주민등록번호
National ID No.

수험번호
Registration No.

비밀번호
Password

고사실란
Room No.

좌석번호
Seat No.

유의사항

본인은 필기구 및 기재오류와 답안지 훼손으로 인한 책임을 지고, 부정행위 처리규정을 준수할 것을 서약합니다.

답안작성시

1. 답안 작성은 반드시 **컴퓨터용 싸인펜**을 사용해야 합니다.
2. 답안을 정정할 경우 **수정테이프(수정액 불가)**를 사용해야 합니다.
3. 문 답안지는 컴퓨터로 처리되므로 훼손해서는 안되며, 답안지 하단의 타이밍마크(▮▮▮)를 찢거나, 낙서 등으로 인한 훼손시 불이익을 받을 수 있습니다.

서약

1. 답안은 문항당 정답을 1개만 골라 1와 같이 정확히 기재해야 하며, 필기구 오류나 본인의 부주의로
2. 답안을 본문은 정답을 1개만 골라
3. 문 답안지는 컴퓨터로 처리되므로 안되며, 답안지 하단의
4. 답안은 문항당 정답을 1개만 골라 1와 같이 정확히 기재해야 하며, 필기구 오류나 본인의 부주의로 잘못 표기한 경우에는 답 관리위원회의 OMR판독기의 판독결과에 따르며, 그 결과는 본인이 책임집니다.
5. 감독관이 확인이 없는 답안지는 무효처리됩니다.

Good ● Bad ◐ ◑ ◉ ✕ ◓

TEPS

Test of English Proficiency
developed by
Seoul National University

응시일자 : 20   년   월   일

〈부정행위 및 규정위반 처리규정〉

1. 모든 부정행위 및 규정위반 적발 및 이에 대한 조치는 TEPS관리위원회의 처리규정에 따라 이루어집니다.

2. 부정행위 및 규정위반 행위는 현장 적발 뿐만 아니라 사후에도 적발될 수 있으며 모두 동일한 조치가 취해집니다.

3. 부정행위 적발 시 당해 성적은 무효 화되며 사안에 따라 최대 5년까지 TEPS관리위원회에서 주관하는 모든 시험의 응시자격이 제한됩니다.

4. 문제지 이외에 메모를 하는 행위와 시험 문제의 일부 또는 전부를 유출 하거나 공개하는 경우 부정행위로 처리됩니다.

5. 각 파트별 시간을 준수하지 않거나, 시험 종료 후 답안 작성을 계속할 경우 규정위반으로 처리됩니다.

성   명 (성·이름순으로 기재)

	성																				명												
EX	H	O	N	G							G	I	L								D	O	N	G										

단체구분

학생 ◯   일반 ◯

질문란

1. 귀하의 TEPS 응시목적은?
ⓐ 입사지원   ⓑ 인사고과
ⓒ 개인실력측정   ⓓ 입시
ⓔ 국가고시 지원   ⓕ 기타

2. 귀하의 영어권 체류 경험은?
ⓐ 없다   ⓑ 6개월 미만
ⓒ 6개월 이상 1년 미만   ⓓ 1년 이상 3년 미만
ⓔ 3년 이상 5년 미만   ⓕ 5년 이상

3. 귀하께서 응시하고 계신 고사장에의 만족도는?
ⓐ 0점   ⓑ 1점
ⓒ 2점   ⓓ 3점
ⓔ 4점   ⓕ 5점

4. 최근 2년내 TEPS 응시횟수는?
ⓐ 없다   ⓑ 1회
ⓒ 2회   ⓓ 3회
ⓔ 4회   ⓕ 5회 이상

성명   서명

학력

졸업   수료·재학

초등학교
중학교
고등학교
전문대학
대학
대학원

전공

인문
사회과학·법학
경제학·경영학
어문
자연과학
공학
의학·약학·간호학
교육
음악·미술·체육
기타

직업

공무원
고시준비
교사
군인
의료인
자영업
학생
회사원
무직
기타

직종

사무직
기술직
전문직(교수·교원·의약)
전문직(법률·회계금융)
기능직
영업
상품판매
단순노무
서비스
기타

직책

임원
부장
차장
과장
대리
계장
사원
인턴
기타

TEPS

Test of English Proficiency
developed by
Seoul National University

수험번호 Registration No.

성명 Name
한글
한자

문제지번호 Test Booklet No.

감독관확인란

청 해 Listening Comprehension

문 법 Grammar

어 휘 Vocabulary

독 해 Reading Comprehension

주민등록번호 National ID No.

수험번호 Registration No.

비밀번호 Password

고사실란 Room No.

좌석번호 Seat No.

서 약

본인은 필기구 및 기재오류와 답안지 훼손으로 인한 책임을 지고, 부정행위 처리규정을 준수할 것을 서약합니다.

유 의 사 항

답안작성시

1. 답안 작성은 반드시 **컴퓨터용 싸인펜**을 사용해야 합니다.
2. 답안을 정정할 경우 수정테이프(수정액 불가)를 사용해야 합니다.
3. 본 답안지는 컴퓨터로 채점되므로 인되되, 답안지 하단의 타이밍마크(Ⅲ)를 찢거나, 낙서 등으로 인한 채점시 불이익이 발생할 수 있습니다.

4. 답안은 문항당 정답을 1개만 골라 ❶와 같이 정확히 기재해야 하며, 필기구 오류나 본인의 부주의로 잘못 표기한 경우에는 당 관리위원회의 OMR판독기의 판독결과에 따르며, 그 결과는 본인이 책임집니다.

Good ❶ Bad ◐ ◑ ⊗ Ⓥ

5. 감독관의 확인이 없는 답안지는 무효처리됩니다.

TEPS

Test of English Proficiency
developed by
Seoul National University

응시일자 : 20　　 년　　 월　　 일

성명

성명	영문
	서명

학력 / 전공 / 직업

학력	전공	직업
초등학교	인문	공무원
중학교	사회과학·법학	고시준비
고등학교	경제학·경영학	교사
전문대학	자연과학	군인
대학	의학·약학·간호학	의료인
대학원	어학·문학	회사원
	음악·미술·체육	자영업
	기타	학생
		회사무
		기타

(중졸이하 / 재학·졸업)

직종 / 직책

직종	직책
무역	임원
의료	부장
자영	차장
건설	과장
언론	대리
품질·진료	계장
교육	사원
전자·행정	인턴
생산·설비	기타
서비스	
기타	

단체구분

학생 ◯	일반 ◯

질문란

1. 귀하의 TEPS 응시목적은?
ⓐ 입사지원　ⓑ 인사고과
ⓒ 개인실력측정　ⓓ 국가고시 지원
ⓔ 기타

2. 귀하의 영어권 체류 경험은?
ⓐ 없다　ⓑ 6개월 미만
ⓒ 6개월 이상 1년 미만　ⓓ 1년 이상 2년 미만
ⓔ 2년 이상 3년 미만　ⓕ 3년 이상

3. 귀하께서 응시하고 계신 고사장에 대한 만족도는?
ⓐ 0점　ⓑ 1점　ⓒ 3점
ⓓ 2점　ⓔ 4점　ⓕ 5점

4. 최근 2년내 TEPS 응시횟수는?
ⓐ 없다　ⓑ 1회　ⓒ 3회
ⓓ 2회　ⓔ 4회　ⓕ 5회 이상

성 명 (성 · 이름순으로 기재)

성	명	G	I	L		D	O	N	G
EX	HONG								
A	B	C	D	E	F	G	H	I	J
K	L	M	N	O	P	Q	R	S	T
U	V	W	X	Y	Z				

TEPS

Test of English Proficiency
developed by
Seoul National University

수험번호
Registration No.

성명
Name
한글
한자

문제지번호
Test Booklet No.

감독관확인란

청해 Listening Comprehension

(answer bubble grid, questions 1–60)

문법 Grammar

(answer bubble grid, questions 1–50)

어휘 Vocabulary

(answer bubble grid, questions 1–50)

독해 Reading Comprehension

(answer bubble grid, questions 1–40)

주민등록번호
National ID No.

수험번호
Registration No.

비밀번호
Password

고사실란
Room No.

좌석번호
Seat No.

서 약

본인은 필기구 및 기재오류와 답안지 훼손으로 인한 책임을 지고, 부정행위 처리규정을 준수할 것을 서약합니다.

답안작성시 유의사항

1. 답안 작성은 반드시 **컴퓨터용 싸인펜**을 사용해야 합니다.
2. 답안을 정정할 경우 수정테이프(수정액 불가)를 사용해야 합니다.
3. 본 답안지는 컴퓨터로 처리되므로 훼손해서는 안되며, 답안지 하단의 타이밍마크(❚❚❚)를 찢거나, 낙서 등으로 인한 훼손시 불이익이 발생할 수 있습니다.

4. 답안은 문항당 정답을 1개만 골라 ❶과 같이 정확히 기재해야 하며, 잘못 표기한 경우에는 관리위원회의 OMR판독기의 판독결과에 따르며, 그 결과는 본인이 책임집니다.

   올바른 표기: Good ●
   잘못된 표기: Bad ⊙ ◐ ◑ ⊗ ⊘

5. 감독관이 확인이 없는 답안지는 무효처리됩니다.

TEPS

Test of English Proficiency developed by Seoul National University

응시일자 : 20 년 월 일

성명	영문
	서명

학력

학력	재학·휴학 졸업·수료
초등학교	
중학교	
고등학교 중퇴	
고등학교	
전문대학 중퇴	
대학교	
대학원	

전공

인문 / 사회과학·법학 / 경제·경영학 / 자연 / 어학·어문 / 교육 / 의학·약학·간호학 / 예능·미술·체육 / 기타

직업

공무원 / 고시준비 / 교사 / 군인 / 의료인 / 자영업 / 학생 / 회사원 / 무직 / 기타

직종

직책

단체구분

학생 ◯ 일반 ◯

질문란

1. 귀하의 TEPS 응시목적은?
   a 입사지원 b 인사정책 c 개인실력측정 d 입시 e 국가고시 지원 f 기타

2. 귀하의 영어권 체류 경험은?
   a 없다 b 6개월미만 c 6개월 이상 1년 미만 d 1년이상2년미만 e 2년이상 f 5년이상

3. 귀하께서 응시하고 계신 고사장에 대한 만족도는?
   a 0점 b 1점 c 2점 d 3점 e 4점 f 5점

4. 최근 2년내 TEPS 응시횟수는?
   a 없다 b 1회 c 2회 d 3회 e 4회 f 5회 이상

성명 (성·이름순으로 기재)

	성				명							
	EX	HONG	G	I	L	D	O	N	G			

각 칸: Ⓐ Ⓑ Ⓒ Ⓓ Ⓔ Ⓕ Ⓖ Ⓗ Ⓘ Ⓙ Ⓚ Ⓛ Ⓜ Ⓝ Ⓞ Ⓟ Ⓠ Ⓡ Ⓢ Ⓣ Ⓤ Ⓥ Ⓦ Ⓧ Ⓨ Ⓩ

〈부정행위 및 규정위반 처리규정〉

1. 모든 부정행위 및 규정위반 적발 및 이에 대한 조치는 TEPS관리위원회의 처리규정에 따라 이루어집니다.

2. 부정행위 및 규정위반 행위는 현장 적발 뿐만 아니라 사후에도 적발될 수 있으며 모두 동일한 조치가 취해집니다.

3. 부정행위 적발 시 당해 성적은 무효 화되며 사안에 따라 최대 5년까지 TEPS관리위원회에서 주관하는 모든 시험의 응시자격이 제한됩니다.

4. 문제지 이외에 메모를 하는 행위와 시험 문제의 일부 또는 전부를 유출 하거나 공개하는 경우 부정행위로 처리됩니다.

5. 각 파트별 시간을 준수하지 않거나, 시험 종료 후 답안 작성을 계속할 경우 규정위반으로 처리됩니다.

Memo

Memo

TEPS의 절대기준

넥서스가 공개하는 서울대 TEPS 가장 최신 기출문제

넥서스 기출문제집

2010년 최신판

대한민국 현존 가장 최신 TEPS 기출문제 대공개

TEPS 공식 강사가 전하는 고득점 핵심 전략

전천후 TEPS 체질화를 위한 비법 특강 600개

기출 빈출어휘집 무료 증정

서울대 텝스 관리위원회 제공 최신기출 시크릿

서울대학교 TEPS관리위원회 문제 제공 · 손진숙 해설 | 456쪽 | 20,000원(MP3 CD 1장 · 기출 빈출어휘집 포함)

서울대 텝스 관리위원회 최신기출 1000

서울대학교 TEPS관리위원회 문제 제공 · 양준희
해설 | 28,000원(MP3 CD 2장 · 별책부록 포함)

유형별로 분석한 NEXUS TEPS 기출 800

서울대학교 TEPS관리위원회 문제 제공 · 문덕
해설 | 25,000원(카세트 테이프 3개 포함)

TEPS 기출문제집 1~3

각 권 서울대학교 TEPS관리위원회 문제 제공 |
1권, 2권 18,000원(CD 2장 포함) 3권 19,000원
(CD 2장 포함)

넥서스 TEPS
진품 교재 리스트

**TEPS 기출문제와 전략이 있으면
TEPS 1등급 가능하다!**

서울대학교 TEPS관리위원회, TEPS 전문강사, 넥서스 TEPS연구소가 탄생시킨
영역별·점수대별·전략별 TEPS 매뉴얼

TEPS 공략 No. 1 ★
기본기부터 다진다

**TEPS 내실을 위한 초중급 알짜 코스
전문강사들의 노하우 공개!**

How to TEPS Starter
성경준 지음 | 25,000원(MP3 CD 1장 및 부록 포함)

How to TEPS L/C·R/C
L/C 전지현 지음 | 21,500원(카세트 테이프 별매)
R/C 송영규·김정민 지음 | 19,500원

**서울대 기출문제 완전 공개, 출제 유형별 적응 훈련을
위한 교재**

서울대 텝스 관리위원회 제공 최신기출 시크릿
서울대학교 TEPS관리위원회 문제 제공·손진숙 해설 | 20,000원(MP3 CD 1장 포함)

서울대 텝스 관리위원회 최신기출 1000
서울대학교 TEPS관리위원회 문제 제공·양준희 해설 | 28,000원(MP3 CD 2장 포함)

유형별로 분석한 NEXUS TEPS 기출 800
서울대학교 TEPS관리위원회 문제 제공·문덕 해설 | 25,000원(카세트 테이프 3개 포함)

**서울대 기출문제 완벽 복원
현존 TEPS 영역별 대한민국 최다 문제 수록**

How to TEPS 시험 직전 리얼 시리즈
청해 넥서스 TEPS연구소 지음 | 19,500원(Dictation Book·MP3 CD 1장 포함)
문법 장보금·쎄니 박 지음 | 14,000원(TEPS 문법 핵심 비법 포함)
어휘 근간 예정
독해 근간 예정

TEPS 어휘 분야 1위

TEPS 어휘 정복을 위한 4주 완성 프로젝트
난이도별로 골라서 학습하는 맞춤식 어휘집

How to TEPS VOCA 2nd Edition
김무룡 · 넥서스 TEPS연구소 지음 | 12,800원 (MP3 CD 1장 포함)

TEPS 공략 No.2 ★ 전략적으로 접근한다

TEPS 초보 탈출을 위한 기본기 형성
청해 · 문법 · 어휘 · 독해 각 영역별 기초 지식 모음집

How to TEPS intro 시리즈
청해 강소영 · Jane Kim 지음 | 22,000원 (MP3 CD 1장 포함)
문법 넥서스 TEPS연구소 지음 | 19,000원
어휘 에릭 김 지음 | 15,000원
독해 한정림 지음 | 19,500원

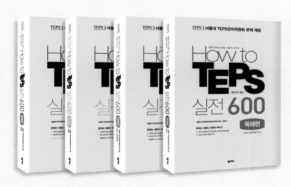

TEPS 600점 이상 획득을 위한 기초 전략 모음
청해 · 문법 · 어휘 · 독해 각 영역별 전략 마스터키

How to TEPS 실전 600 시리즈
청해 서울대학교 TEPS관리위원회 문제 제공 · 박경숙 | 19,500원 (MP3 CD 1장 포함)
문법 서울대학교 TEPS관리위원회 문제 제공 · 이대희 | 17,500원
어휘 서울대학교 TEPS관리위원회 문제 제공 · 넥서스 TEPS연구소 | 15,000원
독해 서울대학교 TEPS관리위원회 문제 제공 · 정성수 | 19,000원

TEPS 800점 이상 획득을 위한 마지막 통과 과정
청해 · 문법 · 어휘 · 독해 각 영역별 고득점 지침서

How to TEPS 실전 800 시리즈
청해 강소영 · 서인석 지음 | 22,000원 (MP3 CD 1장 포함)
문법 김태희 지음 | 15,000원
어휘 넥서스 TEPS연구소 지음 | 12,800원
독해 한정림 지음 | 22,000원

● 넥서스 수준별 TEPS 맞춤 학습 프로그램

기출·어휘
모든 점수대

서울대 기출문제

기출문제집 1·2 | 서울대학교 TEPS관리위원회 문제 제공 | 272쪽 | 18,000원 (CD 2장 포함)
기출문제집 3 | 서울대학교 TEPS관리위원회 문제 제공 | 272쪽 | 19,000원 (CD 2장 포함)
NEXUS TEPS 기출 800 | 서울대학교 TEPS관리위원회 문제 제공·문덕 해설 | 580쪽 | 25,000원 (카세트 테이프 3개 포함)
서울대 텝스 관리위원회 최신기출 1000 | 서울대학교 TEPS관리위원회 문제 제공·양준희 해설 | 628쪽 | 28,000원 (MP3 CD 2장 포함)
서울대 텝스 관리위원회 제공 최신기출 시크릿 | 서울대학교 TEPS관리위원회 문제 제공·손진숙 해설 | 456쪽 | 20,000원 (MP3 CD 1장 포함)

어휘

How to TEPS VOCA 2nd Edition | 김무룡·넥서스 TEPS연구소 지음 | 320쪽 | 12,800원 (MP3 CD 1장 포함)
How to TEPS 청해 필수 표현 1000 | 유니스 정지음 | 304쪽 | 15,000원 (MP3 CD 1장 포함)

파트별

고급
800점 이상

How to TEPS 실전 800 청해편 | 강소영·서인석 지음 | 436쪽 | 22,000원 (MP3 CD 1장 포함)
How to TEPS 실전 800 문법편 | 김태희 지음 | 268쪽 | 15,000원
How to TEPS 실전 800 어휘편 | 넥서스 TEPS연구소 지음 | 244쪽 | 12,800원
How to TEPS 실전 800 독해편 | 한정림 지음 | 484쪽 | 22,000원

중급
600~700점

How to TEPS 실전 600 청해편 | 서울대학교 TEPS관리위원회 문제 제공·박경숙 | 408쪽 | 19,500원 (MP3 CD 1장 포함)
How to TEPS 실전 600 문법편 | 서울대학교 TEPS관리위원회 문제 제공·이대희 | 368쪽 | 17,500원
How to TEPS 실전 600 어휘편 | 서울대학교 TEPS관리위원회 문제 제공·넥서스 TEPS연구소 | 384쪽 | 15,000원
How to TEPS 실전 600 독해편 | 서울대학교 TEPS관리위원회 문제 제공·정성수 | 380쪽 | 19,000원

종합서

How to TEPS L/C
전지현 지음 | 552쪽 | 21,500원 (카세트 테이프 7개 별매)
How to TEPS R/C
송영규·김정민 지음 | 592쪽 | 19,500원

초급
400~500점

How to TEPS intro 청해편 | 강소영·Jane Kim 지음 | 444쪽 | 22,000원 (MP3 CD 1장 포함)
How to TEPS intro 문법편 | 넥서스 TEPS연구소 지음 | 424쪽 | 19,000원
How to TEPS intro 어휘편 | 에릭 김 지음 | 368쪽 | 15,000원
How to TEPS intro 독해편 | 한정림 지음 | 392쪽 | 19,500원

How to TEPS Starter | 성경준 지음 | 564쪽 | 25,000원 (MP3 CD 1장 포함)
TEPS 첫걸음 L/C | 유니스 정지음 | 312쪽 | 15,000원 (MP3 CD 1장 포함)
TEPS 첫걸음 R/C | 김무룡·넥서스 TEPS연구소 지음 | 612쪽 | 22,000원 (부록 포함)

실전 모의고사
모든 점수대

How to TEPS mini mini 1 | 서울대학교 TEPS관리위원회 편 | 164쪽 | 9,800원 (MP3 CD 1장 포함)
How to TEPS 실전력 500·600·700·800·900 | 넥서스 TEPS연구소 지음 | 308쪽 | 실전력 500~800 16,500원 (MP3 CD 1장 포함) 실전력 900 18,000원 (MP3 CD 1장 포함)

How to TEPS 시험 직전 리얼 청해 | 넥서스 TEPS연구소 지음 | 296쪽 | 19,500원 (MP3 CD 1장·Dictation Book 포함)
How to TEPS 시험 직전 리얼 문법 | 장보금·써니 박 지음 | 260쪽 | 14,000원 (TEPS 문법 핵심 비법 포함)